FROM
AUTHOR
TO
READER

FROM AUTHOR TO READER

A SOCIAL STUDY OF BOOKS

PETER MANN

Routledge & Kegan Paul
London, Boston, Melbourne
and Henley

First published in 1982
by Routledge & Kegan Paul Ltd
39 Store Street, London WC1E 7DD,
9 Park Street, Boston, Mass. 02108, USA,
296 Beaconsfield Parade, Middle Park,
Melbourne 3206, Australia, and
Broadway House, Newtown Road,
Henley-on-Thames, Oxon RG9 1EN

Set in 11 on 13pt Sabon by
Rowland Phototypesetting Ltd, Bury St Edmunds, Suffolk
Printed in Great Britain by
St Edmundsbury Press, Bury St Edmunds, Suffolk

Library of Congress Cataloging in Publication Data

Mann, Peter H.
From author to reader.
Includes bibliographical references and index.
1. Books and reading.   I. Title
Z1003.M297   028'.9   82-5419
ISBN 0-7100-9089-7   AACR2

For Lucy

CONTENTS

PREFACE

When I first began researching into the readership of books in 1967 I moved from studying people who went to the theatre to studying people who read books. This change occurred (though I have never lost my interest in the theatre) largely because a publisher asked me at that time what I was researching into and when I said it was people who go to the theatre he said, 'Well then, perhaps you could find out who reads books?' I was intrigued by the idea, my publisher colleague (H. L. Schollick of Blackwell's) had access to some research funds, and I was launched into a field of research in which, at that time, hardly anything at all was known.

Since that time I have myself carried out a succession of research studies which have included bookselling as an occupation, people's buying habits and borrowing habits, students and their books, romantic fiction, the publishing of scholarly books and the modern literary novel. Happily, the book trade itself has, over the years, developed its own research interests and has commissioned more and more research, as well as setting up its own statistical surveys. Librarians too have become more research-minded and, to use their jargon, 'user-oriented'. In all then, there is much more research material around today than there used to be, but such is the extraordinary variety of that one thing we call a 'book' that our knowledge is now only making us more and more aware of our tremendous ignorance.

This current book is an attempt to look at the process of communication which is brought about by books, and to do this I have written chapters on authors, publishers, booksellers, librarians and readers. Some of the research material cited is my own, but much of it is drawn from other sources, especially national surveys where they are available. This present book is not a very long one (for book trade reasons) and I would not want any reader who begins reading it to expect that it covers every aspect of all books. Many of its limitations have been prescribed by its length. For example, it is largely about the book position in the United Kingdom and there are few references to the world book market, which is terribly important to authors and publishers. I have restricted myself also to adult books, since my knowledge of children's reading and school books is very limited. I have, too, tended to highlight the 'general' book, especially fiction, rather than specialist books, partly because I have researched more myself in fiction, but also because I had always intended that this book should, as far as possible, be about the general book and its readers, rather than about specialist reading.

I recognise that what I think I have focused on leaves out a lot of important things. Indeed, one problem in trying to write within the length agreed with my publisher has been deciding what can be squeezed in and what must be left out. I hope, nevertheless, that what has finally been put in tells a coherent and interesting story.

I would dearly like to acknowledge the help given to me by people connected with books who have helped me over the past fourteen years and whose encouragement and comments have in various ways helped me towards this book. To try to do this would be hopeless. Publishers, booksellers, librarians, authors and readers have all been generous with interest and their time and I would therefore like to give a blanket thankyou to everyone who has talked or written to me in my research – and they must now number thousands rather than hundreds. But I would mention especially a few people who have been particularly kind and helpful. They must include Peter Stockham, Eric Bailey, Pearl Taylor, Gordon Graham, Christopher Sinclair-Stevenson, Charles Clark, John Hitchens, John and Alan Boon, Julia Mac-Rae and Michael Hyde in the book trade, all of whom always seem to have had time to talk to me and guide me in my work. Martyn Goff, director of the National Book League, has also been a marvellous supporter of my work. In the libraries I am

greatly indebted to many librarians for help, but especially to Bob
Atkins, the director at Sheffield, and his bibliographical services
officer, Mike Hudson, at Birmingham to Brian Baumfield and his
stock editor, Martin Underwood, and at Leicester to Geoffrey
Smith. I would also like to acknowledge the support I have
received from the Booksellers' Association, the Publishers' Association, the Arts Council Literature Panel and the British Library
Research and Development Department, all of whom by grants,
commissions and the ready supply of information have helped
me over the years. At the University of Sheffield I have gained
greatly from hours of discussion with my friend and colleague
Trevor Noble. My wife, herself a librarian and an experienced
bibliographer and editor, will undoubtedly be embarrassed by
my thanking her, not only for putting up with me, but also for her
gentle support and guidance. I am, as always, deeply indebted
to the secretary who typed my handwritten manuscript, Mrs
Valerie Squire, for whom, by now, Linear B must seem child's
play.

P. H. M.
The University,
Sheffield

Chapter 1

THE BOOK AS A MEDIUM
OF COMMUNICATION

'A book's a book'

If you look up the word 'book' in the *Shorter Oxford English Dictionary*, which usually gives a definition which is sufficient for most purposes, you find that a book, in addition to being things such as 'the libretto of an opera' and 'a main subdivision of a treatise', is 'a collection of sheets of paper or other substance, blank, written or printed, fastened together so as to form a material whole; *esp.* such a collection fastened together at the back, and protected by covers; also, a literary composition long enough to make one volume, as dist. from a *tract, pamphlet, essay*, etc.'[1]

This dictionary definition is useful in drawing attention to both form and content. A book is physically a collection of sheets – usually paper ones fastened together and protected by a cover – which do form a genuine unit. But the book is also more than just the collection of paper, it is a social thing in that it is, as the definition says, a 'literary composition'. The fact of being long enough to make 'one volume' is slightly confusing if one starts wondering if the alternatives are half a volume or two volumes, but the crucial distinction between a book and tracts, pamphlets or essays clarifies the difference. A book is simply bigger than these three examples. A 'volume', says the SOED, is 'something comparable to a book' or 'a collection of written or printed sheets bound together so as to form a book', which shows that dictionary definitions can only get one so far and then the explanations become circular. Nevertheless, it is clear that a 'book' has a particular physical form which makes it longer than, say, a pamphlet and that this requires that the person who has written the book has more material to put into it than could be coped with by a shorter form of publication. A book is thus a fairly substantial piece of work whatever the content may be. If it is a work of fiction it could be a novel rather than a short story. If it is a work of scholarship then it is a monograph rather than a journal article.

The importance of this *substantial* aspect of the book must be stressed at the outset because books are not the only way – nor necessarily the best way – to communicate between people. Today a great deal of communication is done by words and by pictures. Even when the *written* word is used, the book has many competitors. Newspapers and magazines can be used for rapid and brief communication. The microfilm and microfiche can compress large amounts of written information into a few square inches. Access to data banks is rapidly providing for obtaining information which is not in conventional 'printed' form at all.

The whole position of the book as a medium of communication in modern industrial society is being challenged and even conventional ways of producing conventional books may be completely altered by new means of composition and what is now called 'on-demand publishing' whereby individual copies of books may only be fabricated as a need for them arises. The importance of technological developments in the media of communication cannot be ignored and the role of the book in modern society undoubtedly will be changed by new technology.

Yet, when one looks around the world and recognises that many countries are still only at an early stage in working towards total literacy, the role of the book becomes even more confusing. Some developing societies, especially in, for example, Africa and Asia, are still moving towards the use of the book, whereas others, especially in Europe and America, are wondering if they are moving beyond it. The ability to read is, of course, so obvious in the use of the book that those of us who live in advanced societies sometimes tend to overlook not only the widespread illiteracy in many countries of the world but also the relatively recent development of what we like to think of as 'literate societies' and the non-use of literacy skills by many people in these societies.

Much of what is written by people who would claim to have 'a love of books' is actually about limited aspects of books as media of communication. The cultural heritage of a literate society can be transmitted from generation to generation in a cumulative way by means of the written, and particularly printed, word. The distinction between these two adjectives is important. So long as a society has developed a form of writing then handwritten manuscript form of communication is possible between the literate population, however small or large that may be. But when multiple copies of any original manuscript can be produced at low cost for a wide readership, and thus a 'book market' created, then the society is transformed. To the sociologist the transmission of a society's culture includes all aspects of the distinctive way of life of that society and this must include not only the 'literary' heritage of fiction, essays, biography and so on but also the scientific, technical, political, legal and economic heritage which is contained in a diversity of written forms.

The book, therefore, is not just the artefact which contains the original thoughts and creative writing of great novelists and poets, it is also the storehouse of technical information, legal decisions, statutes, records and so on which may be not just boring but even completely unintelligible to the non-specialist. The book in itself is, then, merely one particular way of putting together written information for a literate audience or market. Many an advanced research worker in science or technology may rarely read a book for his work – journal articles and research reports are the media he uses most. Many people use the book very little in their leisure hours – they find television, radio, music and conversation preferable ways of filling in their time. What, then, is so special about 'the book'?

Speaking as a specialist in librarianship and information science, W. L. Saunders[2] referred to the book as 'that on-line, real-time random access storage device'. This amusing and perceptive 'definition' of the book puts aside all the emotional feelings which people may have about books and simply sets out the functional advantages of having information available in book form. But Saunders's definition could equally apply to the bound volume of the journal, the short research report or the pamphlet. The book has no unique quality that sets it wholly apart.

Perhaps the aspect of the book which does make it seem to be rather special is the fact that it is produced in quantity and thus the possibility is there for each individual to have his or her own personal copy of a book. Having personal immediate access to a writer's thoughts and work through one's own copy of a book is undoubtedly very convenient and the importance of this *amenity* must not be underestimated. The scholar's *personal* library can be a very important tool for him and the popular stereotype of the great scholar is of a man at his desk surrounded by shelf after shelf of books. That this stereotype may bear very little connection with reality these days is of less importance than the fact that an environment in which books are very evident is thought to indicate high learning. To a certain extent scientists may be exempted from this stereotype since they actually *do* things with incomprehensible glass and electrical apparatus, but for real *thought* a library of books is the obvious setting.

Of course, all knowledge today is cumulative. Every scientist, social scientist or humanist draws upon the findings and the thoughts of his predecessors or his current colleagues the world over. Much of that working knowledge is obtained through the written word and much of this is contained in books. Even today, undergraduates at the older-established universities are said to be 'reading' for their degrees. The one title in universities which is awarded to a scholar for the highest levels of research and nothing else is a 'readership'. Undergraduates, research students, academic staff in higher education, research scientists in public and private institutions are all people who are expected to work in an atmosphere where books are used as an integral part of the information system. Whether or not the person concerned uses his own book or books borrowed from a library is not of great importance. The important thing is that books are a part of the working situation. This fact sets such situations apart from the many other working situations where books have no part to play

4

at all. In many aspects of manufacturing industry, in retail distribution, in many offices and governmental departments the working day rarely requires a person to use a book. Even in work situations where books may have a function there may well be important status differences between those people who use books and those who do not. Thus charwomen and porters in a university work in an institution where books are used a great deal but they themselves are highly unlikely to use them.

When we look at the use of books outside work, in people's leisure time, again we see the book having different functions for different people. For some people evening and weekend reading of books which have nothing at all to do with their work is a favourite pastime and novels, biographies, travel books, books on hobbies and so on may be 'consumed' avidly. By contrast, other quite literate people may prefer to spend their leisure watching television, listening to the radio, going to the cinema, the theatre, the pub, to sporting events or any of a hundred other forms of recreation. In the home some people will have personal libraries of several hundred books and still also borrow regularly from libraries; other people will own no books at all and rarely, if indeed ever, read a book. They may well read newspapers (as most people do) and magazines – but not books.

So the convenience and the amenity of the personal access to information or ideas which is available to every literate person through the medium of the book is not made use of by everyone. Provision and access is widespread and, via libraries, can be said to be virtually universal in this country, but the use made of facilities for buying and borrowing books is highly selective.

It will be an important theme in the later chapters of this book that the balance between supply and demand in the book world is a very difficult balance to attain. Books may be *useful* to many people, but it is by no means common for them to be *necessities*. Books may seem pleasant and attractive forms of leisure for some people; for others they may be the most boring ways of spending free time yet invented. It was Lord Byron who said, 'A book's a book, although there's nothing in't.' For sociological analysis

5

one must go further than Byron and consider quite seriously just what *is* in the book.

Books are different

It is a commonplace within the book trade that 'books are different'. Indeed the whole defence by the trade of the Net Book Agreement whereby retail price maintenance was continued was argued on the grounds that books are different from such goods as soap or cornflakes. But books not only differ significantly from other manufactured goods; they differ between themselves. It is an important aspect of books that each book is unique. It may seem superficially that one book on cookery is just like another or that one modern spy novel is really no different from six others of that genre, but this is not so. Similarities there may well be – and no elementary textbook can avoid some basic features of a subject – but no two books *can* be identical, otherwise it would be inevitable that one author had plagiarised the other's work.

If we consider a few examples of different types of books we can see that books must be different. Some years ago one publisher advertised a new book on gardening with the claim that this book told you all you were ever likely to want to know about gardening. Were this claim literally true then there would be no further need for any other publisher to produce another book on gardening. One sees publishers' advertising or even book reviews which refer to the 'definitive' biography of an eminent person in history. But even this description does not seem to deter new authors and other publishers from producing further books on the same subject. The potential for new books is infinite in a free society – and restrictions on new books are, happily, not imposed by a department of agitation and propaganda through its censors.

In spite of the fact that there *seems* to be so much similarity between certain books the differences are there, though sometimes it requires special skills to appreciate them. For example, if one takes school teaching books which are used in quantity in the classroom by the pupils themselves, it may seem that, shall we say, an introductory book for the teaching and learning of French or chemistry could not be all that different from another one. But whilst both may be tackling the same problem they will most definitely tackle the problem in different ways and the way that appeals most to the practising teacher will gain the larger market. In this particular sector then, the publisher and author must be very much aware of the *needs* of teachers and the *ways* in which they are teaching their subjects because schoolroom books are tools for the use of teachers.

If we look at a totally different sort of book – romantic fiction – we find here a form of novel which, to the outsider who has never read one of them, may seem to be endlessly repetitious. All are about young women meeting handsome men, at first disliking them and then discovering that they love them, with the inescapable 'happy ending' which means matrimony in these cases. Yet the *aficionado* of romantic fiction will be able to distinguish with ease between the novels of two authors whose storylines seem, to the outsider, to be virtually identical. The treatment will be different and this will be apparent to the experienced readers, so the books, to them, will be quite different.

In scholarly books, of course, where the authors are extending the field of knowledge in a particular subject, differences between books are of the greatest importance. In this area the scientist reader expects new findings to be used to extend knowledge and develop theory and the humanist reader may expect new evidence or concepts to be used to develop a new perspective on a subject. So it is not just a case of yet another book on Thomas Hardy, or Gladstone or Shakespeare or Karl Marx; it is a case of at least some new ideas and, it is to be hoped, some new evidence.

Looked at in this way, in which the unique qualities of books, rather than their similarities, are stressed it becomes apparent that every book has something different to say. But, obviously, no one person in the world would ever attempt to read every book that is available for reading. There is no definitive figure for the total books, even in the English language, which could be read, but estimates of the books currently in print in Britain usually give a number of round about a quarter of a million titles. Each one of these books must have been presumed to have some interest for some people otherwise they would not have been written and certainly they would not have been published. What then are the presuppositions that lead to the writing and publishing of all these different books?

Looking through the weekly lists of new books announced in the *Bookseller* is a fascinating, if daunting, activity. *Behavioural Weight Reduction Programme for Mentally Handicapped Persons: Self Control Approach* sounds interesting, though at £11.75 a copy one wonders how many individual people will buy their own copies. However, it might well be bought by specialist libraries and health workers both here and in America, where it was published. *Policing and Punishment in Nineteenth Century Britain* sounds as if it might well be bought by both educational and public libraries as well as students of the law. *The Films of Robert Altman* sounds as if it was written for a specialist readership, as does a book entitled *Guide to the Antique Shops of Britain* selling at £5.95 from the Antique Collectors' Club. *Adventure Camping* at £6.95 should appeal to appropriate enthusiasts, as might *Karate for Self Defence* at only £3.95. *Safer Cancer Thermotherapy* seems a highly desirable publication, whilst *The Development of Libraries in Papua New Guinea* and *Anglo-Saxon Missionaries in Germany* both sound like works of very specialised scholarship. *Dors* by Diana Dors will undoubtedly interest her fans.

The *Bookseller* weekly list gives clear evidence of several things. One is that many books published in this country have originated from other countries – often the USA. A second point is that many books are published by publishers whose names are *not* household ones. And third, and linked to the second point, many books are obviously published for a very specialised and therefore limited readership. The naive reader who thinks of 'books' as being primarily works of fiction – the novels on the public library shelves or in paperback form in the local department store – would have a reasonable amount of searching to do to find ten novels amongst the many works of non-fiction listed each week.

So it is clear (and trade statistics confirm it) that the bulk of titles published are works of non-fiction. In these circumstances the book is primarily a medium for the conveyance of information of one sort or another. That information may be for business, for science, for humanistic scholarship or for personal leisure, but whatever the purpose the book form gives a particular package of information which can be read and which can be retained and referred to at will. For the reader as user, therefore, the book is an information source. For the reader of fiction the book is a recreational object.

Quantities of books

Since 1963 the British book trade has published over 20,000 new titles each year, with an increase in each year except two and reaching a record of 36,092 new titles published in 1980. In addition to new titles each year there are reprints and new editions of already published books and these have been over 7,000 a year since 1967, with a figure of 9,236 in 1978, which was only recently beaten by 10,776 in 1980. This tremendous outpouring of titles is one reason why British publishing has such a highly esteemed place in the world. But the publishing of a *title* gives no indication of the actual numbers of *copies* (or units) of that title which are printed and (it is hoped) sold.

It is remarkable how little appreciation there is outside the book trade of the simple economic fact that if a book is printed only in small numbers then the unit price is likely to be high and if it can be printed in large numbers then the unit price will be lower. Along with this fact there is also the important other fact that a 'paperback' form of binding only reduces the unit cost to a limited extent below that of the casebound version; it is really the larger *print-run* of the paperback that brings prices down. So a copy of, say, a hardback first novel may well be £6 and a paperback edition of a well known writer's novel might be less than £1.50. The difference is largely attributable to the very small print-run of the former and the much larger print-run of the latter – a point to be discussed later in this book.

If this matter of print-run is applied across the whole range of books then it can more easily be appreciated why a scientific monograph may easily cost £20 and a popular autobiography may cost only £6 or £7. The former could well have a print-run below 2,000 copies whereas the latter's publisher might be hoping for a sale of 20,000 or 30,000 copies – and even then, perhaps, a paperback edition to follow. Clearly the market for these copies is of vital importance to both publishers and book-sellers and there is no magic formula which can be applied to tell the publisher what print-run to choose and what retail price to decide upon.

These unanswerable questions arise because it is impossible to forecast with complete accuracy the sale of any one book. The need of readers to *purchase* a book must vary with every title. On the one hand students on a particular course often have a book prescribed as a text, purchase of which is virtually essential. On the other hand no leisure reader is ever actually obliged to buy a copy of a novel. Personal possession of a book by an individual is not very often an absolute necessity. Frequently a book is only needed or wanted for a restricted period of time. In the case of a 'work' book that period of time is as long as it takes to extract certain information from the book. In the case of a 'leisure' book it is no longer than it takes to read the book from beginning to end – or when the reader gives up without completing a full reading.

The question must be asked then, why is it that so many people do actually buy and retain personal copies of books? There is no one clear answer to this intriguing question and if there were the book world would be a duller place. What is apparent is that books are *not* simply media of communication in the way that, say, newspapers or magazines are. The person who never throws away a newspaper is regarded as an eccentric; the person who never throws away a book is more likely to be regarded as a bibliophile – no matter what the resulting motley assortment of books may be.

To *have* books in the home in British society is a mark of social status. The inference to be drawn from the book collection is that the owner of them is a book reader – and to be a book reader is still 'a good thing'. Not to be able to read in our society is a source of embarrassment and shame, as workers on the recent national campaign discovered when they were first trying to contact illiterate people. Illiteracy in our society is not only terribly inconvenient, it also carries with it a stigma and illiterates on television programmes have described the subterfuges they have employed to cover up this fact about themselves. Fortunately illiteracy in our society is not commonplace, even though estimates of as many as 2 million people were at one time made. But, like homosexuals, illiterates rarely advertise their problems and no accurate estimate of their numbers can be made.

Simply being able to read is a skill which gives the young person entry to modern society and achievement in school and subsequently at work depends greatly upon literacy. It is not surprising that parents of young children place great emphasis on the acquisition of reading skills at an early age – even, at times, pressing so hard on their children that schoolteachers have to try to reduce that pressure. It is a commonplace occurrence amongst young parents to hear them boast how quickly their offspring are learning to read. This is one of the first assessable skills which the young child can demonstrate and literacy normally carries greater prestige than numeracy.

So to be able to read is praiseworthy in that it shows success in the early stages of primary education and, as books are used so much within the schools, the reading of books becomes a particularly praiseworthy activity. For the child to show signs of reading for pleasure is an even better thing. There is a rather curious problem which arises, however, at an early stage in life. Having acquired the basic reading skills the child is capable of reading over a very wide range of books. In some cases these books are the tools of school learning, but outside the school there is no set reading curriculum for leisure and choices have to be made. It is here that the child has to learn that there is reading which carries status and reading which does not. Many of the problems in children's reading, and much of the controversy over what should be stocked in children's libraries, revolve round the matter of choosing 'suitable' books for children of all ages. In some libraries an author such as Enid Blyton may actually be banned from the shelves even though it is known that her books are very popular with children.

In school education the *activity* of reading quickly becomes allied with the *subject* of English, which covers a certain amount of English grammar but, certainly in secondary education, is almost synonymous with English literature. Given this pedagogic tradition, having once achieved the ability to read fluently the child associates the act of book reading with a restricted range of selected books, most of which are works of fiction. The fact that reading skills are also used in subjects such as history, geography and, of course, foreign languages, does not detract from the pre-eminent status of English as *the* subject concerned with reading as cultural activity. Textbooks are used in all school subjects and there is an ever-increasing range of project books and other such ancillary tools published for school work today. But only really in the subject of English itself are books used which themselves are adult publications never intended for use in education at the time of writing. This statement must be modified to some degree, since school pupils studying foreign languages will undoubtedly read the adult novels of their chosen subjects, but the real point of importance is that English uses adult fiction as the *material* of study. History, geography, physics, chemistry, biology and the rest may use books written for schools and books written for higher educational institutions – but they are all *educational* books. English alone uses that most cultural manifestation, the novel, as the basic reading material of the course.

Culturally, therefore, our society creates a heritage for children in which fiction – the imaginative form of writing – is accorded a position of high prestige. Books are used at all levels and in all subjects throughout school education, but in no subject except English does the medium of the book and the content of the book come together so closely. In new teaching experiments made in recent years teaching 'packages' have frequently replaced books as the teaching and learning materials. But, as yet, no English 'package' has been evolved which can replace the reading of the novel itself.

In higher education the importance of the book is stressed by students having a component part of their grants allocated for the purchase of 'books, stationery and equipment', though the details of the amount within the total grant are no longer divulged to the students themselves. The university library itself has a dominant place within the university and, of course, 'reading lists' place emphasis on the use of the right books. It must be recognised that the further the student goes in his studies the further he (or she) is likely to move away from books towards the use of journals and research reports, but nevertheless there are many humanities and social science subjects where books predominate throughout the whole undergraduate course. Simply to carry books around the university often seems to give students confidence and one does at times wonder if they believe that the information in the book will in some miraculous way transfer itself via hand, arm and shoulder into the head – just as one does sometimes wonder if people believe that photocopying a page of a book is as good as reading it. It was Thomas Carlyle who claimed that 'the true university of these days is a collection of books'.[3] Carlyle has been dead nearly a hundred years, but one understands what he meant and many an academic would like to agree with Carlyle even if, perhaps, universities have changed rather a lot since his day.

In all, therefore, we have a society in Britain today where 'book learning' still carries high prestige and affords high social status. It is essential to be able to read, it is desirable to be able to read well, it is creditworthy to read voluntarily and it is prestigious to have an occupation which is associated with reading. Our 'book culture' confers a status on people who work with books, so that to be an author is a mark of status – even though it may bring a negligible financial reward. To be in book publishing as an occupation is desirable – as long queues of young graduates wanting to enter this occupation testify. Even if publishing is questionably still 'an occupation for gentlemen' it is still vastly over-subscribed by would-be entrants. To sell books is still more special than to sell groceries – even though the profits may be pitifully low – and to be a bookshop proprietor is a much more middle-class status than is that of grocer, haberdasher or vendor of garden implements. To work as a librarian is so terribly respectable that young lady trainees at library school have been known to try to keep their specialism a secret from young men so as not to prejudice their chances of acquiring boyfriends. In all, it is difficult to find an activity or occupation associated with books which is not status-conferring to some degree and certainly it is very difficult to think of discreditable activities associated with books apart from the writing and selling of pornography – and even that has its defenders.

Given, then, the high place accorded to the book in modern society it is desirable to understand just what books *are for*. What do they *do*?

The functions of books

If we accept that books can play an important part in our lives, it is useful to consider what our lives are made up of. One basic sociological distinction which is very relevant to books is that made between work and leisure. Without going into all the conceptual problems of defining work and leisure, it can be said that most sociologists of leisure accept that we all of us spend the twenty-four hours of the day in activities which can broadly be categorised as sleep, work and leisure. Sleep is the simplest category to deal with as the person asleep is unconscious and can be said therefore to be inactive. We also spend a certain amount of time each day dealing with our bodily functions, bathing, washing, brushing our teeth and so on. Such activities are a part of our physical routine and can, for the most part, be noted and set aside. For the rest of our working hours we are engaged in activities of many kinds, nearly all of which are of some social significance even if we may be alone at the time.

In an exchange economy of an advanced kind, such as we live

in, we take part in activities known as work. Even if the activity does not produce profits or wages work is not difficult to recognise. The housewife cleaning her house, shopping, cooking meals, rearing her children and washing and ironing is undoubtedly working just as much as is her husband on the car assembly line or in the insurance office. Equally the housewife happily crossing off her numbers in the bingo hall is just as much at leisure as is her husband painting his pigeon loft and then going for a drink with his mates at the pub. There is no need to be over-pedantic about the principal distinctions between work and leisure; any normal person knows the principal differences.

But there are subtler distinctions which must be considered which are of importance in understanding the functions of books in society, since books themselves have so many different purposes and possible uses. Definitions of leisure usually refer to the use of *time* which is free from obligations, time in which a person can choose what to do. Now very little human behaviour is totally 'free' from some social relationship or obligation. If I choose to watch a rugby match on television on a Saturday afternoon I may well consider that this is a 'free' choice activity which has no relationship to my job in a university. But I might also wonder if I ought not to be using this 'free' time for reading sociological treatises which will help advance my career or – more likely – I might wonder if I ought to be digging the garden as my wife would like me to do so that she can plant vegetables. The fact of there being so many choices open to me is typical of the leisure situation. I can voluntarily decide to use my so-called leisure time to extend my working week; I can engage in activities which benefit other people and acknowledge my responsibilities to them; I can do what *I* feel I want to do for my own personal pleasure. But even if I choose to use my leisure for myself I have a wide range of different things I can choose from. I can undertake leisure activities which will develop physical or mental skills – such as carpentry or chess. I can engage in do-it-yourself activity to improve the value and comfort of my house. I can join a sporting club and combine developing skills with social activities. I can offer my services to a voluntary social group and engage in social work or ecological conservation. I can become active in a local political party and try to change society. The possibilities are innumerable and all of them can be subsumed under the general heading of 'leisure'.

It is noticeable that in most of the examples given above the person engaged in a form of leisure activity is doing something more than just 'filling in time'. Many leisure activities result in the development of personal skills that have nothing whatsoever to do with a person's work. Indeed some sociological theories suggest that people frequently choose leisure activities which are highly unlike their work so as to add variety to their lives. Thus the office worker compensates for his indoor sedentary occupation by sailing or camping. The factory worker compensates for his noisy and dirty work environment by digging his allotment. On the other hand, people can use their work skills in their leisure pursuits. The mechanic can spend his spare time building up an old car; the administrator can help organise a local charity. Whatever the leisure may be in itself, the person engaged in it frequently develops new interests and new skills. For such activities books are often useful accessories – indeed they can even be basic necessities.

The market for 'leisure' books has increased greatly with the affluence of modern society and the time people have available for leisure activities. Any bookshop or library today will have a wide selection of books catering for leisure activities. Activities such as gardening or cookery are dealt with in many books in ways which go far beyond the simple keeping down of weeds or just filling empty stomachs. Leisure today is sophisticated and often technical and these developments are reflected in the books which are published.

But not all leisure is creative in an active way. Some activities develop aesthetic appreciation of culture and many books on art are published. The so-called 'coffee-table' book may be regarded as a 'primer' for the uninitiated on English country houses, Persian carpets and Dutch paintings. Highly specialised books on aspects of warfare are so frequently published today that there must be a ready market for them outside the professional student.

Extension of knowledge in both general and specialised fields is an important aspect of leisure for which book publishing does a great deal.

In the field of fiction one comes to a vast area of books, indeed a category so important that most public libraries make a fundamental distinction in classification, cataloguing and shelving between fiction and non-fiction, with fiction only rarely subdivided into any other form than 'alphabetical by author'. The reading of fiction (and to a certain extent the reading of biography and modern history) can be looked at in two ways. Some novels, usually referred to as 'literary' novels, are serious works of imagination which aspire to being genuine contributions to thought and culture. Dealing, as they do, imaginatively with the personal problems of characters in special social situations, the novels are a commentary on contemporary or historical society. The story may be fiction, but the problems, the emotions, the values and the relationships are derived from reality and are used deliberately to comment on that reality. To read a 'serious' novel, therefore, is to accept a form of stimulus which will require the reader to undertake an intellectual form of exercise if any real benefit or understanding is to be gained. Literary novels do not set out simply to entertain and give enjoyment; indeed they can be tremendously depressing. Nevertheless these books are intended for leisure-time reading by a general readership – not for scholarly analysis in the seminar room.

What is often referred to as 'light fiction' is normally regarded as having a different function. This type of book, well exemplified by the romantic novel and the modern spy/adventure story of the James Bond type, is written for entertainment and escapism. Being of less serious purpose it receives less critical attention and gives less prestige to its authors and publishers, though earnings for these people from sales can be extremely lucrative. 'Popular fiction' is much more 'time-filling' in its function and is rarely considered as having any creative or intellectual element. This attitude probably does less than justice to some of the genre of popular fiction. The stories themselves may not result in the reader questioning the basic philosophical principles on which society rests but they can be helpful in showing young women how to cope with romantic situations and young men how to behave in sophisticated settings. The novels exaggerate reality, of course, but then so do more serious novels. J. W. Saunders[4] claims that

> It is an experience to come across a new book for the first time, no matter how cheap and shoddy wiser men may find it. If, for instance, one has never read one of the glossy modern thrillers in which the heroes are always taking three fingers of rye and the blonde heroines are voluptuous in bar after bar the book adds something to experience, not much perhaps, but something. The experience diminishes to zero with further reading. But for a little while the author concerned has made a small contribution to literature.

Robert Escarpit[5] defines literature according to a criterion of what he calls 'the search for gratuitousness'. He says that, 'Any work which is not functional, but an end in itself, is literature. Each act of reading which is not a means to an end, one which satisfies a cultural, non-utilitarian need, is literature.'

Popular fiction, however, has an important function in providing for people who are seeking relaxation in their reading. The busy housewife with small children and a husband to care for is more likely to find recuperative provision in a romantic novel where things go right than in a serious novel where a busy housewife with small children and a husband discovers he is committing adultery, has just lost his job and has developed cancer.

To describe fiction simply in two categories as 'serious' and 'light' is to run the risk of creating a false dichotomy and suggesting a polarisation which is not actually found in reality. Certainly there are very serious novels which, by means of a fictitious story, have a great deal to say about human relationships and social structures. Equally there are quite trivial romantic novels and adventure stories which say little about the major personal or social problems of modern or historical society. But between these two extremes there lies a large number of books which do a certain amount of both, and publishers, booksellers, librarians and readers are all aware of the importance of novelists who are good storytellers, who can hold a reader's interest, portray believable people and situations and provide some cerebral stimuli for the reader. Fiction is a vast category of books and the social implications of the whole range of fiction have never been satisfactorily explored. This neglect of looking at the total range of this type of writing is in itself an interesting sociological phenomenon. The students of 'literary' culture normally ignore 'popular' culture whereas the very limited amount of study of popular culture that does take place usually examines that category as if it existed totally separate from the literary variety. A *total* understanding of the functions of fiction is therefore not achieved. One would certainly agree with Saunders's[6] argument that

In the last analysis literature is valuable because it gives insight into human nature and insight, unlike literary structure, is not readily definable in absolute terms but it is not conducive to a better understanding of the effects of literature to restrict the definition of that word too narrowly.

In addition to fiction certain types of non-fiction books are very popular for leisure reading and here autobiography, biography and memoirs are an important category. Once again one can see the sensitivity of public librarians to popular taste in reading rooms where a general category of 'biography' is separated from all the other categories of non-fiction. Thus, if the Dewey decimal cataloguing system has been adopted for non-fiction, biography will be exempted from such cataloguing and will perhaps be labelled on book spines as 'B' for biography. Since the best of biographical writing tells a good story it is not surprising that this type of book is very popular with the general reader. Of course, books of this type may be of considerable historical and political importance, but looked at sociologically one can see how biography (especially in the form of autobiography and memoirs) enables the reader to look into, and even share vicariously in, the life of an interesting person. Not only does the reader learn about events in history (and particularly in very recent history) but also he learns to understand the position of individuals in social settings, the problems they face, the motivations for their actions and the arguments they use to resolve dilemmas and problems.

The function of the book in people's leisure lives is, then, extraordinarily widespread. By the one medium of communication – produced and distributed in a fairly standardised way – the reader can learn new skills, can be introduced to new facts, can become a more knowledgeable citizen of the whole world, can be stimulated to both thought and emotion over fictitious depictions of real-life problems and situations and, in general, can be helped to create a total persona which is much more highly developed and genuinely 'aware' in the best sense of that word.

It would, however, be ridiculous to claim that the book is the only form of communication which offers all these facilities and there are serious competitors today in the communication of information and imagination. In the printed word alone both newspapers and magazines are very serious competitors which cater extremely skilfully for the person who has either little time or little inclination for the volume of content which the book offers. Newspapers today, particularly the more serious ones, contain so many feature articles that the general reader may feel that he has sufficient information on, say, the problems of central Africa without going to a book-length analysis. In the magazine world both general and specialist magazines in this country offer a range of coverage which leaves few loopholes. Whilst economics, politics, literature and so on are well covered by general magazines, specialist interests in sports, recreation and hobbies seem at times to be even over-comprehensive. It was noticeable when skateboarding came to its brief zenith of popularity that there were three or four magazines quickly on the market to cater for this very specialised interest. It is a rare sport or hobby indeed that does not have its own magazine – or two, or three.

Whilst newspapers and magazines may be regarded as competitors with books they nevertheless are regular free advertisers of books through their review columns. It is an interesting social phenomenon that virtually all quality newspapers and magazines give appreciable space to book reviews. Even popular newspapers and magazines usually have some space for book reviews and specialist magazines virtually always carry some reviews of new books within the specialism. All reviews are a form of free publicity (discounting the cost to the publisher of giving away the copy of the book) and it is usually accepted in the book trade that even a bad review is better than no review since at least the book does get mentioned.

Newspapers and magazines review cinema, theatre, television, and radio too, but the book page still has an importance and a cachet which the others do not have since a 'literary editor' does not have to work single-handed as do most theatre or cinema critics. Selection of books for review sometimes causes controversy as to why some are reviewed and others not and the reviews themselves can create minor storms in the book world if it is felt they are prejudiced or spiteful. But whatever the reviews themselves may or may not do the fact remains that newspapers and magazines, without charge, deal with books in a serious way and try to promote their sale and readership. Clearly the newspaper editors and proprietors do not see themselves in direct competition.

Since radio and television operate largely in people's leisure time their functions *vis-à-vis* books are very important since all broadcasting reaches such large audiences. Radio today has changed its function greatly since the full development of television coverage and peak audiences are reached at mealtimes during the day rather than in the evening. A great deal of popular radio now, especially musical programmes, is simply 'sound wallpaper' which provides background music requiring very little attention, but both local and national stations can, and do, provide specialised programmes for particular interest groups. Radio, however, is very limited by being sound only and so television is able to provide for a much wider range of interests where visual evidence and examples are crucial. A series of coaching programmes in virtually any sport will come over magnificently on television whereas on radio they would have no impact. Darts and snooker have both become favourite television sports in recent years; on radio their impact would be minimal.

Television has not only become a prime medium of communication in society today, with an average weekly viewing of nearly twenty hours per person per week in this country, it has also been a great stimulation of new interests, particularly in the leisure field. Showjumping is one of the clearest examples of a very specialised and minority participant sport which has commanded wide television audiences because of its visual impact. Rugby union, which comes over very well on the television screen, is said to have increased in general spectator popularity very considerably in the last five years or so largely because of the presentation of top level games on television. Much of television viewing is a passive activity; few people who watch showjumping or rugby union are active participants themselves. But television does cater for the smaller numbers of active people by means of coaching and advice programmes given at off-peak times.

In all these ways it could be argued that television (especially) and radio are competing very successfully with the written word for people's *time* in their leisure hours. Certainly it is virtually impossible to watch a television programme and read a book at the same time. Yet book publishing, buying and borrowing have actually been stimulated by television. When books are serialised on television their sales shoot up – as the *Forsyte Saga* and the *Poldark* series showed. Where books are produced, by the BBC itself or with other publishers, to complement programmes the results can be bestsellers – as with Sir Kenneth Clark's *Civilisation* and Alistair Cooke's *America* and David Attenborough's *Life on Earth*. The BBC itself, of course, is now a substantial publishing house with its books and pamphlets to accompany its many leisure programmes on foreign languages, cookery, etc., and all these ventures add new books to the list of publications.

The essentially practical nature of many books associated with television programmes contrasts interestingly with the programmes on television which actually deal with books themselves. These book programmes tend to focus rather more on authors and their 'literary' work, and the people involved in reviewing new books are usually drawn from the more restricted literary field of interests. Nevertheless these programmes most definitely do review books in a conventional way and authors, titles, publishers and prices are all clearly demonstrated to the viewer. So, whilst radio and television may in one sense be seen as competitors with books they also stimulate people's interest in books and lead to the publication of more new books.

To a much lesser degree cinema may also be said to be both a competitor with books and a stimulation of them. Although cinema declined greatly with the development of television and can never hope again to reach the popularity it enjoyed in the 1940s, it is still a medium which enjoys considerable mass audiences and 'the book of the film' is always a hopeful publication just as books about films, film directors and film actors published for 'cinema buffs' have a certain appeal. The fact that some of these books seem to gravitate to the remainder bookshops would indicate that their appeal is less than the publisher had hoped for, but again the example shows that one medium generates production in another medium.

The part that books play in people's lives is well illustrated by the list of 'bestsellers' which appears on the inside of the back cover of the *Bookseller* each week. This list, which is carefully compiled in collaboration with the *Sunday Times*, lists both hardbacks and paperbacks. Taking as an example the issue of 25 July 1981, the hardback list consists mainly of non-fiction books covering a wide range of interests. Two small dictionaries from Collins and Oxford are highly placed. There are four books relevant to the royal wedding. The *Michelin Guide to France* is well placed and sport is represented by the 1981 *Wisden*, a book called *Test Match Special* and Mrs Borg's memoirs *Love Match*.

In its paperback list there is more fiction, but the top of the poll is *Not! The Royal Wedding* and there are two books on how to solve Rubik's cube, a cookery book and the official royal wedding guide.

These lists – and the week chosen is a reasonably typical one – indicate the wide variety of interests that books cater for and, of course, the 'bestseller' lists do not deal with specialised highselling books such as school books, manuals, technical books and other such works which can sell in hundreds of thousands over time. The book, then, is a medium of communication which is extraordinarily adaptable for a huge range of contents. It can be used to teach small children to read; it is used at every level and in every subject in education; in many occupations it provides essential reference material in convenient form; in recreation and leisure it provides for every conceivable interest. The book as a package of printed material is, then, an extraordinarily flexible and convenient medium of communication.

But for books to act as media of communication there must be functionaries who work together to enable the person who has something to communicate to present the person being communicated to with the object, the book. Thus books require authors to write them, they require publishers to put them together in book form, they require booksellers to offer them on the market and they require purchasers who will buy them. These purchasers may be librarians who are going to lend them to other people as well as individual people buying for themselves. In the next chapter we look at the first stage in the process and examine the role of the author.

Chapter 2

AUTHORS

What is an author?

As we have already seen, books themselves are of infinite variety and it must therefore follow that the writers of books demonstrate a great diversity too. In this chapter it is my aim to differentiate between types of authorship so as to distinguish between authors analytically. It is quite pointless to write of 'authors' as if that term and that term alone is reserved for the writers of literary fiction. Amy Cruse wrote, 'We can all be readers, though few of us can be great writers.'[1] She could equally have written that many of us can be published writers but few of us can be great writers. Indeed, it is difficult to know quite what a 'great' writer is. Undoubtedly Charles Dickens would qualify as a leading British novelist, but would the most successful writers of school textbooks qualify? Would Marguerite Patten or Fanny Craddock qualify with their cookery books? Would Harold Robbins, probably the world's most highly rewarded novelist, qualify?

So much of what is written about authors is restricted to discussions of men and women who wrote or write serious literary fiction that there is a great danger of distorting the role of authorship, its functions and its rewards and losing sight of the fact that only a small minority of books published are serious literary fiction. Leaving aside the writing of journal articles, pamphlets, research reports and the like, any person who writes a book of any sort is an author. What is relatively rare in the total world of publishing is the person who is an author *and nothing else*. Being an author frequently is not a full-time occupation upon which a person is wholly dependent for his or her living.

Authors of most academic and scientific books are academics or scientists for whom book writing can be an accepted part of their work, but their salaries continue to be paid whether or not they write books – though in the United States academics do seem to be under greater pressure to publish something, and books certainly help. Writers of books for school use are often practising teachers and only a handful of very successful authors can contemplate giving up teaching and living from their book royalties.

Medical books are usually written by practising doctors, law books by lawyers (in practice or at universities). Hundreds of unsuccessful children's books are written by practising mothers and only a few are lucky enough to have their work published. Adult novels seem to be written by everyone under the sun – perhaps in the belief that everyone has a book inside him (or her). Analyses of earnings of members of the Society of Authors have tried to concentrate upon those people who do depend principally on their books for their living, but even in these surveys it has proved difficult to show where authors are *wholly* dependent on their book writing. Many engage in other forms of writing which earn them money and some are wives with husbands who have regular earnings.

The situation is obviously very complicated because books themselves are complicated, so it is best to begin this analysis by attempting some form of categorisation of authors. For some authors the writing of books is an occasional activity almost incidental to their main activities in life. For other people it is a highly professional and demanding occupation upon which their livelihoods depend. Between these two extremes lie a variety of other types of people, all of whom are authors.

Why write?

Sociologists interested in the media of communication, like sociologists in many other fields, have tended to look at aspects of social culture by using polar types. On the one side is 'high culture' catering for the intellectual elites, on the other side is 'mass culture' catering for an undiscriminating mass audience of 'consumers'. Much of the argument about the development of the media[2] uses these polar types for analysis of change in modern society and some people argue that the spread of communication has debased high culture whereas others argue that it has raised the lower levels and created completely new and better forms of culture compared with, say, the nineteenth century. Wilensky[3] has argued that 'the good, the mediocre and the trashy are becoming fused in one massive middle mush' and that 'intellectuals are increasingly tempted to play to mass audiences.' Much of his criticism is aimed at the development of television but the argument is equally applicable to books. Escarpit[4] has argued that in any society it is the cultured group which exercises literary judgment and therefore the critics of any forms of high culture are 'connoisseurs', or experts in a restricted field of interest. It follows from this that for a writer to succeed with a book the readers, as critical recipients of the book, will give carefully considered reasons as to why they do or do not like the book. By polar contrast the book for the mass culture reader, the 'consumer', simply aims to please and it is sufficient for the reader simply to say that he (or she) likes the book without having to give any carefully analysed reasons for that like.

If we turn around this type of analysis and apply it to the author rather than the reader then it can be claimed that the author of the high culture book is writing for his (or her) peers, for knowledgeable readers who will be expected to judge his books by high standards agreed amongst an elite group who have prior knowledge of the subject area. If the author is, however, writing for a mass culture 'market' of as many readers as possible, then judgment is made simply according to the pleasure that the book gives to the reader. The dichotomous model upon which this type of analysis is based suggests that high culture is innovative and 'shapes' a total social culture, whereas mass culture is conservative and merely reflects the present state of a culture.[5] So for an author to be writing for a high culture readership there is an expectation that he will have something new to contribute to thought. The mass culture author does not question cultural values or suggest new ideas, he is merely interpreting the present state of affairs to a wider audience.

The typical sociological use of polar types, dichotomies and contrasted opposites is useful up to a point, but requires further analysis if it is not to mislead. By contrasting polar types there is a danger of, first, suggesting that the two poles are in conflict with each other and, second, that there is no linking 'middle ground' between them. The fact that high culture is said to have existed before the modern media of communication brought about the development of mass culture is followed by an argument that mass culture is threatening to replace high culture. This argument is attractive to those sociologists who subscribe to conflict models, but it is not necessarily true. Both high culture and mass culture can, and I would argue do, exist side by side within the one society. Serious novels and light fiction are still published just as the media of radio or television can be used to broadcast both classical music and pop. Mass culture does not necessarily drive out high culture.

What has actually happened in the last century and a half is that society itself has been transformed, the media of communication have developed and affected everyone's lives and the total amount of cultural material available throughout society has multiplied many times over. There is today culture of all sorts at all levels – high culture, middle-brow culture and mass culture – and there is no evidence to show that the one sort pushes out the other. Society has increased its ability to consume a vastly greater amount of cultural output through its increased material standard of living, through education and literacy, through the expansion of leisure time and through a technological revolution which has brought new media of communication into every home.

Watt[6] has suggested that the complement of the mass public is the professional author and he feels that this point was actually reached in the eighteenth century. Certainly a mass public creates a demand for communication which makes possible new occupations and books are no exception. But it can also be argued that developments in knowledge also create a demand for more knowledge and the interpretation of knowledge to wider audiences, so that scholarly writing and technical writing are also supported and encouraged. Creativeness in all fields of activity results in an interest, a demand for more and eventually a market. So authors of all sorts find an audience so long as freedom to communicate remains an undisputed right.

It can therefore be seen that between writers and their readers there is a very complicated relationship. Looked at from the author's point of view a book may be an act of originality of thought on his (or her) part in which the content of the book itself is what concerns him, not whether there is likely to be a market for it or whether readers will actually 'like' the book. At this end of the continuum one has the novel which the author writes because he has an idea that must be put down on paper, the work of scholarship where the author has a new theory or a new perspective to propound. The relationship here is between author and content. At the other end of the continuum is the form of hack writing typified by the poorest quality of adventure stories (often mildly pornographic), romances or westerns where authors write again and again to a standard formula with no attempt at creativity simply because they are writing for what is believed to be a certain market. Here all power lies with the reader and it is the author's task to provide the content which has been predetermined. Perhaps this type of writing is more common in the USA where the home market is greater than in Britain, but certainly it is the sort of book writing which is sometimes referred to as 'factory' style. But between these two extreme polar types there lies a whole range of books and authors operating at all sorts of different levels. There is the work of the very competent and literate novelist who is not avant-garde or the current darling of the critics, but is certainly regarded as a professional and imaginative writer. There is the biographer or historian who can write at an acceptably scholarly level but who is not necessarily advancing the frontiers of knowledge but is rather interpreting the advanced scholarship to a wider audience. There are the straightforward 'craftsmen' writers who can produce a competent technical manual or perhaps a school book in which the information is correct, though not necessarily at a very high level, and presentation of that information is done with great skill.

Within the ranks of authorship therefore there are many types of author and it is invidious to claim that any one sort is necessarily 'better' than another. Undoubtedly novelists, especially writers of high culture novels, enjoy high prestige in our society because imaginativeness and sensitivity are accorded high status in the book world, but a good populariser of a difficult subject, a person who can write well and stimulate many people to take an interest in a new subject, certainly has very special skills which are worthy of high praise.

We can see from the analysis so far that there seem to be three important factors which can help us understand the functions of authorship. First there is the author himself (or herself) and his ideas. Second there is the content of the book he writes, the form in which his thoughts are expressed on paper. Third there is the readership of the book, the people who together make up a market for the book.

Without going back to the dichotomous polar types we can now develop a model (Figure 1) which is much more flexible and which enables us to have a continuum upon which authors can be placed, whether in fiction or non-fiction, according to the purposes of their writing.

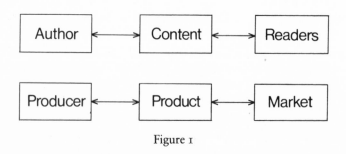

Figure 1

All authors of books are initiators in a chain of communication. The author has something he wants to communicate to someone via the medium of the book. What the author writes becomes the content of the book and thus the product of his labour. When the content is put together and actually published in book form as a product it is read by the readers who are thus the ultimate market. It does not matter at this stage in the analysis whether the books as products are actually bought by libraries or private individuals; that problem will be dealt with later.

Novelists as authors

The various real-life forms of the author–content–reader relationship can be illustrated by a number of examples. Perhaps the most extreme form is the first serious novel written by a completely unknown author. It is virtually unheard of for such an author to be concerned with the problems of readers and markets. Indeed most first-novel writers have no idea of what book publishing entails in finding markets. In the serious novel the author has an intense concern with the content of the book, but the mechanics of publishing it are not his (or her) concern or even interest. Novelists, being writers who create books from their own imagination, are frequently introspective people who can cope with the solitariness of fiction writing. After all, the world itself has no actual *need* of new novels in a utilitarian sense. Technological progress, the international economy, the third-world development – none of these would actually be hindered if novels ceased to be written. But novels do appeal to the imagination and novelists are people of imagination who often feel that they *must* write. All fiction publishers know that there are far more people who feel they must write than there are editors who feel they must publish their novels. The very fact that so many novels are written and rejected demonstrates how little thought so many authors have given to their potential readers. It is as if the novelist is frequently writing to himself in the first place and merely hoping that somewhere out there are other people who would like to know what he is saying.

The very successful novelist Margaret Drabble had some extremely interesting things to say in an interview with an

American researcher, Peter Finchow,[7] who compiled a whole book of interviews with modern writers. Margaret Drabble said of novel writing, 'One does it for oneself. If you're paid so much the better.' Later she added, 'I'm not terribly interested in selling. I get terribly embarrassed when publishers start talking about sales, because this isn't what I'm after. What I'm after is writing something that I can take seriously myself.' Margaret Drabble is a novelist who is successful both by literary and commercial criteria. She satisfies the literary critics who take her work seriously and generally approve of it and she satisfies a large public who buy her books in hardback and paperback editions and thus provide her with royalties, which led her to comment, 'I make more money than I ever expected out of writing novels. I'm absolutely staggered by the fact that one can earn a decent living out of it. It's amazing to me. I wouldn't have expected it.' Perhaps it is a little unworldly of Miss Drabble to be so surprised at the income a very successful novelist can achieve, but the important point in her statements on novel writing is that she obviously writes *in the first place* for herself. It is clear that her novels must satisfy *her* first before anyone else comes into her thoughts at all. In this way she is a very good example of a writer whose prime concern is the relationship between herself and the content of her novels. To be applauded by critics and to have large numbers of readers who provide her with large royalties are of secondary importance.

Margaret Drabble is still able to say, 'I don't think that a novelist should expect necessarily to earn a good living out of writing novels, because one can't pretend it's either a full-time activity or exactly a service to the community if one does it.' Her reference to the part-time nature of novel writing is an important one from a person who does write regularly and successfully but who also says, 'I do write a lot of things for money. I write scripts or reviews or articles for money. It's got to be something I'm interested in. I wouldn't *just* write something frightfully boring for it. But a novel: I would *hate* to think I was writing to get royalties, because that would compromise me.' This statement is most helpful since it clarifies the situation that faces most serious novelists. First it is rare for a novelist to regard novel writing as a completely full-time occupation and second most novelists have sources of income in addition to those their novels produce for them.

Beryl Bainbridge is an author who at the present time (1981) is enjoying considerable success with her novels both critically and commercially. Her novels are relatively short and she has said that she only spends about two weeks a year actually writing a book. For her the time spent in being an actual writer is thus very small. Angus Wilson[8] discussed his early days as an author with Peter Finchow and said that, 'I had to write my first novel in the four weeks of holiday that I had from work.' At that time Angus Wilson worked in the British Museum library. For many years Iris Murdoch, one of the country's leading serious novelists, was a lecturer in philosophy and a fellow of an Oxford college. Only in recent years has she given up her academic post.

The situation is, then, that few serious novelists actually live wholly on the royalties from their novels. Even the successful ones usually have income sources from reviewing, writing articles for commercial magazines, broadcasting, lecturing and other forms of communication activities. The writing of serious literary fiction is not often found to be either a full-time occupation which excludes completely any other sort of work or a complete source of self-supporting income. The developments in the media of communication have increased the possible sources of income for novelists who are good communicators in other ways and the situation is rather different from pre-war days when living costs were lower and writers would try to get by on very small incomes from writing. Richard Hughes told Peter Finchow[9] of his experiences in the 1920s. 'Not long after I left Oxford a London publisher offered me a small fixed income provided he could have my first novel when it appeared.' Hughes says that this subsidy was enough to keep him 'along with what I was already making through book reviewing and amateur play royalties and so on'. He explained that Charles Prentice, who was then head of Chatto & Windus, 'had the sound idea of investing some of the "backlist" income in new writers in the hope that they too would become his backlist one day. If he lost on some of them, he lost on some of them – that was part of the game.' It is certainly not a game in which many literary publishers can afford to indulge today.

Pamela Hansford Johnson[10] told Peter Finchow of her experiences in the 1930s when 'it was very much easier for a first novelist to get going. . . . In the thirties if you were a first novelist and you sold fifteen hundred copies, then your publisher was delighted with you. . . . If you managed to sell about four thousand copies you could live on it.' Unfortunately she does not say how many novels would be required to be published in a given period to produce a living from royalties, but certainly 4,000 copies seems a small number.

The above extracts from Finchow's interesting and revealing interviews all show novelists who were (and are) serious writers accepting the problems of deriving a living income from their novels but not being *primarily* concerned with the commercial aspects of their work. Indeed it is a constant theme running through all Finchow's interviews that the writers were determined to write no matter how difficult it was for them to make that work commercially viable. It is also clear from the interviews cited and others in his book that most novelists began by writing whilst they were in other occupations, hoped to have their books published and only at a much later stage when their books were bringing them reasonably substantial monetary rewards were they able to contemplate giving up their other occupations and becoming 'full-time' writers. Even when this stage took place the authors were often buttressed in their novel writing by other pieces of freelance writing. It should also, of course, be mentioned that any published writer benefits from the sale of foreign language rights in his books and the sale of film rights can be especially lucrative.

It can therefore be argued that the serious novelist has a rather professional attitude to writing in that he (or she) wishes to be paid so as to do his writing rather than doing his writing for pay. As several authors commented to Finchow, their greatest need was for *time* to do their writing. Pamela Hansford Johnson argued that, 'historically it's simply not true that a writer must devote himself exclusively to his craft' and she cited Dickens, Fielding, Chaucer and Trollope to support her case. But some authors do find that they need at least 'time off' from their normal occupations to enable them to devote themselves wholly at least for a time to their writing and it is for these people that temporary incomes by way of subsidies and bursaries from the Arts Council Literature Department are of considerable help, even though the wisdom of such bursaries is questioned by some writers who have managed to achieve success without them.

Nevertheless, successful or unsuccessful, the literary novelist is a prime example of the person who writes because he (or she) wants to write. In some instances that need to communicate can be fitted into a person's life as a 'spare-time' occupation. For others it can become so overpowering that evenings, weekends and holidays are not enough. But whatever the position may be about securing an income above the starvation line the clear emphasis is on the relationship between the author and his book. The book is written for the author, not for a calculated readership which will produce a book market which will earn the author a fortune. If that miracle does occur (as it does from time to time – and Richard Adams's *Watership Down* which began life as a children's book is perhaps the most extraordinary example in recent publishing history) then that is good news for the author, but not news he really ever expects to hear.

Authors of scholarly monographs

The second example of a polar type author for whom the content is all is the author of the scholarly monograph. In some ways the serious novelist and the scholarly author are similar. They are both creative writers in the sense that they have new things to say. The scholar's work is based on his (or her) researches, but even so his theoretical ideas are imaginative ones, pushing back the frontiers of knowledge, as the saying goes. The scholarly author is also primarily concerned with content rather than reader, though here there is an important difference. The novelist is writing in some ways to himself but hoping that there is a readership who will be interested in the fiction he creates. The scholar is writing to a degree to satisfy himself but he is always conscious of his readership since they will inevitably be his peers in the subject of his specialisation. So whilst both novelists and scholars may expect to be reviewed by elite critics the novelist's critic is a rather 'general purpose' reviewer who can only use criteria for judgment which are largely intangible and subjective. The scholarly author will expect to be reviewed by experts in his subject whom he will have to satisfy by objective criteria. Beyond the limited number of critics who review the book he will also have to satisfy all his readers of his scholarship otherwise he will find his book the object of critical papers submitted to journals and his professional reputation could be questioned. The comparison between novelist and scholar is an interesting one, since reactions to the serious novels and the monographs are never simply of liking or disliking. The novel reviewer must always give reasons for his approval or disapproval of the novel under review and he must show himself to be knowledgeable about modern literature so that his critique is acceptable to serious readers. The monograph reviewer also gives his reasons for approval or disapproval but his expertise in the subject of the book must be considerable if his review is to be judged a worthy appraisal of it. However, authors do not write simply for reviewers, important though they may be, and scholars write monographs to inform their colleagues of the advances they have made in their special fields of scholarship.

For the scholar there are more alternative ways of communicating than simply the book. Many eminent scholars, especially in science and technology, publish mainly in journals or through special research reports of a length shorter than the conventional book, and rarely, if ever, write books. Indeed, for much scholarly communication the volume of writing required to justify publication in book form may be much greater than is appropriate for the research work. Also publication in book form is often a slower business than publication in scholarly journals and when a scholar wants to publish his (or her) latest research findings (especially in experimental work) speed of publication is of overriding importance.

It is therefore customary for scholars to publish their current work in journal articles and research reports first and then to bring together a larger amount of work in book form. This generalisation has, of course, many exceptions and it is common-place to find scholars in the humanities and some of the social sciences working on long-term projects with the express inten-tion of publishing all the work in book form as the primary form of publication.

For the scholar such as the historian or philosopher the book then becomes a medium for informing his (or her) fellow workers in his specialism of his personal findings, thoughts, empirical evidence and theoretical conclusions. The relationship between author and content is intense, since the scholarly author must first convince himself of the worth of his arguments before he submits them to his peers. So far as his 'readership' is concerned they are a group of equals in that they will be interested in the content of his work and not in him personally. The object of publishing in book form is simply a means to an end – the end being the dissemination of information and ideas in a convenient-ly packaged form. The readers as 'a market' for the book will be the concern of the publisher but not of the author since the author will not be especially concerned with monetary rewards for his book. This is not to say that scholarly authors are so altruistic that they are prepared to write books for nothing; indeed in my own researches I have come across situations where authors felt deeply about the way that publishers had treated them financial-ly. But virtually all scholarly authors are in some form of employment, most of them in institutions of higher education, where they are expected and encouraged (even required) to publish the results of their researches. The authors are always allowed to retain their book royalties as additional to their salaries and, of course, publications are important when com-petition for promotion is involved.

Thus the scholarly author working in a university or polytechnic has strong incentives to publish and the monetary reward, though usually quite small for a limited print-run mono-graph, is a pleasant additional perquisite. In a study I carried out[11] into seventy-five scholarly monographs in a wide range of sub-jects published by five different firms, and in which I asked about the books of both authors and publishers, I found that the desire to communicate one's findings to fellow researchers was always the dominant reason for writing at all, but many authors did also positively enjoy writing, especially in book form.

One scholar, a professor in a scientific subject, who had both written and edited books wrote:

As an academic I naturally regard research and 'scholarly activities' (e.g. writing reviews and books) as important parts of my job. In fact the whole concept of academic life involves communication of the special knowledge which one inevitably gains to other people of various kinds – colleagues, graduate and undergraduate students and, if possible, to the public at large. . . . As for the authorship of books – a book is a more flexible and less restricted medium of communication than a paper in a scientific journal. One can often state things at greater length in a book, one does not have to tie up all the loose ends of an argument so concisely and one can deal with other people's work. . . . Also, like many academically-minded people, I love books for their own sake and have always wanted to write a few – though I see myself as a research worker rather than a 'professional writer'. . . . A book can also express one's personality in a way that a specialised scientific paper cannot really do. No doubt this is an egocentric idea, but I suspect that most authors feel like this at heart.

This eminent scientist added that it would be hypocritical to ignore the fact that authors do receive payment but as he wrote,

The financial rewards for academics are perhaps not so important with the present punitive taxation. But the editorship and writing of books (provided they are reasonably good ones!) does very properly carry some prestige in academic life and may help one's prospects and promotion.

This statement from a very experienced, senior academic covers most of the key features of the writing of monographs and is particularly illuminating about the way that the book as a medium of communication is an attractive way of writing to the scholar. The love of books and the enjoyment of writing them is by no means uncommon amongst scholars and shows a certain similarity with some novelists. The lack of expectation of high monetary rewards is also similar to that of most serious novelists.

An author of a book in the humanities described his purpose as follows:

My motive in writing the book was simply, to put it immodestly, that its contents seemed true and worth saying to other scholars in the field and to such wider audience as it might reach. While the book is aimed principally at specialists it seemed to me – and to the publishers – that it could be of interest to others who are prepared to work hard to understand what is in fact an area of some general concern.

This statement emphasises the possibility of a book on a humanistic topic being read by both the author's peer group and a slightly larger audience too, but the people on the fringe would have to work hard for themselves to develop high enough standards of judgment for the book to be of any value to them. The first sentence from the author stresses the importance of the *content* and makes it clear that the readers must adjust themselves to the content; there is no question of the content being modified or diluted in any way for the readers.

A further author explained how he hoped his work would appear first to the advanced scholars but might also filter through to students. He wrote,

Although it is unfashionably elitist to say so, I must admit that the intended *readership of my book is, as the blurb says, 'scholars and advanced students'. But naturally I would wish that university teachers would pass on to their students the message of my work, should they think it worthwhile.*

Note that this author hopes that his work will eventually get through to the students even if they themselves do not necessarily read his book at first.

A different type of book, but one which has a purpose quite similar to that of the monograph, is the advanced-level review study, normally edited by one or perhaps two scholars, with contributions from a number of specialist researchers. One such book was desirable because, as the editor put it, 'Twenty years of work by a large number of researchers had established a new, or at least considerably modified, understanding [of the topic].' The book put together the work of over a dozen people 'with the object of providing a comprehensive statement for scholars who want to review the work of the last twenty years or so'. This book looked backwards but with the object of providing a stock-taking so that scholars could continue to go forward. Again the subject matter was the key feature and the readership was expected to be small and knowledgeable.

Whilst many people seem to have a strong urge to write serious fiction no one is, so far as one can see, ever in a situation where there is any sense of compulsion to write novels. In the scholarly world postgraduate students are required to present theses for their higher degrees and, especially in the humanities and the social sciences, there is often a possibility of a scholarly monograph arising from the PhD thesis (or even sometimes a research-based master's degree).

Postgraduate students who gain full-time academic staff posts sometimes see their PhDs are useful bases for books, sometimes they are encouraged by supervisors or professors to develop them into books so as to establish themselves in their lectureships and, probably in most cases, there is a combination of the author wanting to publish as well as feeling a certain pressure on him to publish. But most PhDs are not written as books; they may be too narrow in scope or they may be so full of detail as to frighten off book publishers. One author said of his book,

It bears a strong relationship to my PhD thesis but it is not the same work. It covers a longer historical period and has other additional material, all compiled after the PhD was presented. . . . Naturally it is a technical work, easy reading I hope, but only for cognoscenti.

This book is probably a good example of the doctoral thesis being broadened in scope with the maturity of the scholar but still restricting itself to a narrow audience. A different case was the young lecturer whose PhD supervisor was an editor of a series for a publishing house and who made it clear to the postgraduate student that he hoped the thesis could also be a book. The student had to reduce the length of the thesis to make it acceptable as a book but the work was actually accepted as a book before being accepted as a PhD, which is an unusual state of affairs. Nevertheless in both these cases the monographs which were published were works of scholarship refereed by academic editors working with the publishing houses before they were accepted and intended primarily for a restricted readership of fellow scholars. Although both young lecturers hoped to establish reputations for themselves with their books the object of the exercise was to contribute to the advancement of knowledge rather than to reach a large and profitable market for the book.

Books with a wider readership

In analysing serious literary fiction and scholarly monographs as examples of books where the content is all the emphasis has been on books in both fiction and non-fiction in which the authors write at a high level of imagination or scholarship for a readership which is known to be limited by either cultural or scholarly factors. Many novels and non-fiction books are written, however, which, whilst still being regarded as showing skill in their writing, are not so limited in their readership appeal. It is easier to think of non-fiction books which are still of good technical or academic level but are aimed at disseminating known information rather than advancing knowledge itself. In these instances one can think of authors who can write extremely well and yet not sacrifice their standards. Authors such as the late Jacob Bronowski in science, Kenneth Clark in art and A. J. P. Taylor in history are good examples of excellent high-level scholars who can also write 'popular' books. Below their levels of scholarship are numerous writers who can produce textbooks, guides, manuals and a host of other sorts of books which translate new developments in subject areas into a form which can be read and understood by the lower-level student or the intelligent layman.

But the relationship between author, content and reader also allows for consideration of books in fiction which fall into a similar category though, clearly, the categorisation is not so easy to make since literary criticism is not as objective as scientific or humanistic criticism. Nevertheless it is possible to place authors on the continuum suggested by the analytic model according to certain reasonably objective criteria. For example, novels which are short-listed for literary prizes, such as the Booker Prize, are judged solely according to their literary merit and not in any way according to their market potential. The novels are submitted to the organisers by the *publishers*, not the authors, which is an interesting point, since publishers hope to increase sales through the publicity arising from the winning of a prize. The author, however, has not written the book with the aim of winning a prize; to the author the book is an expression of his (or her) imagination conveyed in book form.

It is quite impossible to say, though, of every novel that this one is 'literary' and this one is not. There is no simple dichotomy which can be applied in an area where personal critical views can differ so widely. But simply by looking at the book pages of serious newspapers and magazines it is evident that the selection for review amongst the many novels published each year shows a high degree of tacit agreement between literary editors and/or their book reviewers. At the present time of writing new novels by authors such as A. N. Wilson or John Fowles will certainly be given serious consideration on any literary page. But besides the very 'literary' authors there will also be many writers whose books do not get as much consideration in reviews but who are nevertheless regarded as serious novelists of a slightly less 'literary' stature. It is invidious to make comparisons which suggest that the more literary writer is 'better' than the less literary one (and classifications, whether vertical or horizontal, make it difficult to avoid some suggestion of ranking) since no two novelists ever can be said to have exactly the same aim in their writing, nor to write in exactly the same style. Clearly, though, the literary work tends to be much deeper in its analysis of personalities, motives and events than does the less literary work which may well tell a story extremely well but not go into such depth of analysis of the characters. Today especially the literary novel tends often to be a psychological exercise, at times extremely introspective, with a limited time scale and a lack of action. By contrast the more 'popular' novel tends more to a wider canvas of action and a more outgoing cast of characters. It could be called more social than psychological, though one must take care here not to confuse social with sociological, since the latter type of novel can also be extremely analytical. To help in the contrast the literary could be described generally as analytical and the less literary as more descriptive.

The ability to write well in the descriptive mode without simply producing film scenarios with two-dimensional characters is not a quality given to many novelists and it is a skill which is welcomed by both publishers and readers and results in a book which can be sold in reasonable numbers in bookshops and will be sought after by public librarians. The good 'middle-range' novelist, if one may use that term, is therefore an author with a wider appeal normally than the very serious 'literary' novelist but the wider appeal is not attained, or even sought, through a dilution of quality; it is simply that this type of writer has a different sort of skill. The result may be less cerebral and challenging to the reader's understanding but it is not an inferior product – it is simply different.

Examples of novelists who come into this category are likely to be found on sale in hardback editions in larger branches of W. H. Smith and through general book clubs, both of these types of sales outlets being very discriminating in the novels they select for sale. This is not to say that novelists such as Graham Greene and Iris Murdoch who are held in the highest critical esteem are *not* sold through these outlets, which indeed they are in good number; the point is that authors in the middle range who are *not* accorded the highest literary prestige do appear on sale in these outlets.

Similarly in the non-fiction category there are many authors of great skill in their writing who are interpreters of scholarship rather than scholars themselves. They are writers who do not themselves produce new primary information but can use that primary information for their own books. Again, there is considerable skill in being able to distil other people's work into a good textbook, guide to literature or review of a historical period.

Authors who work on this type of book are very varied indeed and may include academics, teachers, journalists and authors whom it would be reasonable to designate as 'professional' authors who earn at least the majority of their income from their books. This category of writing can virtually overlap with scholarly writing in some cases and, in my own researches into scholarly publishing, I have come across books in the subject of law particularly which can be called textbooks but which are also considerable works of scholarship carrying high prestige as well as good royalties. But also in law there are minor textbooks which are basically aids to student courses in which the skill of the author in knowing what to omit is considerable. I have even come across student books in law and medicine which are almost a form of 'underground' literature in that they are well known to booksellers and students but are never referred to in the lecturers' reading lists. But these books are really at the other end of the continuum in that they are written for a definite purpose of passing examinations and for a carefully defined market.

At the point of overlap with scholarship was the case of an author who explained that his book was intended in the first place for university students but he also had in mind a much larger public of 'intelligent readers' (which did not necessarily exclude students) who cared about the subject of his book. In this particular case, where the book was in a humanities subject, it could be intelligible to what this author called 'civilised men' who were of a sufficient level of culture.

At a more practical level were two books on particular topics of law, both written by academics with clear and limited aims. One author said he had attempted 'to present a pretty complicated subject in a compact and, I hope, readable form'. The other said he had tried 'to write a book which was up-to-date, simple and accurate'. So far as the publishers were concerned both had succeeded in their objectives. The books combined accuracy with intelligibility and filled a place where they were needed for law education. The matching of the author's special skills with a presumed demand for a product involves the expertise of the publisher a great deal with this type of book since it is likely to be printed in much larger numbers than the monograph and, if successful, further revised editions can be hoped for in future years.

But authors themselves can be important in initiating books, as was exemplified by a scientist who began teaching a specialist introductory course some years ago and gradually, over the years, got together what he felt was a very good set of lecture notes. He also then realised that the only textbook on his topic was not British and, in his opinion, not very good, so he drafted an outline of what he would write and, with advice from a colleague, contacted a publisher who accepted his plan. The book is a success and has brought him several thousand pounds of royalties each year since publication. He was not writing primarily for the monetary reward when he started on the book but its sales have certainly raised his living standards and he has not in any way prostituted his scholarship. In contrast to this book was a student text which the author claimed was written in six weeks entirely for royalties, makes no contribution to scholarship and was written simply for a student market. The author certainly does know his subject and used his educational skills in selecting what was needed for the students in the subject at the appropriate level. But he clearly had no great pride in the work he had done which, he claimed, was simply done for the money. This is a clear example of writing for an assumed market in a very calculated way, but if the book fulfils a useful function for the students of this subject at the appropriate level then the author should congratulate himself on having done a useful workman-like job. It was clear, though, that this author felt that the job had been below his dignity and that he regarded the royalties more as compensation for the work rather than as reward.

In the middle range of authorship there is, then, quite a wide band of writing stretching from the scholarly to the market-orientated and authors may themselves be scholars aiming for a wider readership but still at a high level or they may simply regard themselves rather as hacks putting together books for the money. For this category of book the skills of the author *as a communicator* are of considerable importance and these are skills which normally carry less prestige than the skills of imaginativeness or scholarly research. To be able to present *other* people's ideas is not as status-conferring as to present one's own. Thus historians or scientists who can popularise their own work and who have an undisputed status as scholars (Sir Mortimer Wheeler was a good example) can also disseminate other scholars' work in a more popular way without necessarily losing status, but *only* to be able to communicate and interpret other people's findings and ideas is clearly felt by some authors to be working at an inferior level.

Perhaps the real point of difference in this form of writing is between the author as a *creator* of a book, in which case the emphasis is clearly on the *author* function in the model, or on the *book* itself which is to be written by the author, in which case the emphasis has moved more to the *product* in the model. It therefore follows that with greater attention being paid to the book as a product the role of the publisher will be greater and the consideration given to the market for the book will loom larger in everyone's thinking.

It is therefore not surprising to find that with this category of non-fiction book the publishers will quite commonly anticipate ideas for books themselves and will look around for authors to commission. It is here that the 'professional' author of political history, biography and so on will be asked by the publisher to consider writing a new book on a chosen topic. This also explains why it is not uncommon to discover two books on the same topic being published almost simultaneously as two publishers had independently noted a forthcoming centenary of a birth, death or historical event. Such commissioning of books of this sort does not in any way imply that the author is working as a hack. In fact the use of the term 'commissioned' to describe books of this sort can be misleading. It frequently happens that an author who has already been published by a house on a particular subject is encouraged to think of further possible subjects for books and the publisher's editors themselves take an active role in thinking of new ideas. The result, not infrequently, is that when the subject of the book is finally determined and the way of dealing with it in book form has been agreed, neither author nor editor is quite sure who contributed what to the final decision. With books which are closer to the scholarly type than the market-orientated there is quite frequently a major contribution from scholar editors who are not full-time members of the publishing house but who act as series editors, consultants, readers and referees for the house. Particularly in the case of series, their ideas for who to commission to write what can be of the greatest importance to the publishers.

In a similar way with books for a more general readership for which scholarly editors are not necessarily employed, the publishing editors will have their contacts with authors of known interests and capabilities and an interchange of ideas will produce commissioned books of a good level of expertise and reliability but intended for the 'intelligent layman' rather than the specialist scholar. For these books the author's ability to communicate an interest in the subject is vitally important since the market for the book is difficult to predict. There is not, on the one hand, the small but (the publisher hopes) reasonably predictable market as for the scholarly monograph, nor is there, on the other hand, a definite intention to aim the book at a mass market with a high print-run in paperback form. The middle-range book may become a bestseller, in both fiction or non-fiction, but if it does this is rather more of a pleasant surprise than an expectation.

A useful example of a non-fiction book of this sort is the autobiography (often ghosted) or the biography of a leading sportsman or woman or of a stage or film actor or actress. Books of this type are usually closer to the market type than the author type, but some autobiographies do actually have quite serious ideas to communicate. There is a fairly good library market for such books in hardback editions and sales through bookshops to interested individuals can be quite good. If the title is selected by a book club this helps boost the print-run and overall sales. Not many of these books are expected to go into paperback editions though and the selling lifetime of the book is expected to be limited as it has its day and is then replaced by the next 'personality's' book. But every now and then a general book of this sort hits the jackpot and becomes a genuine bestseller. David Niven's amusing but very lightweight autobiography *The Moon's a Balloon* is an excellent example of this phenomenon and it was impossible for the original hardback publishers to forecast the tremendous success of this book. In effect, the book started its life rather more as a light entertainment middle-of-the-range hardback autobiography but popular acclaim turned it into a huge mass-market paperback success. David Niven and his publishers, Hamish Hamilton, clearly hoped for some success with the book but could not have predicted the enormous degree attained.

In general then, the books in the middle range can extend across a continuum from those which are almost in the category of being 'author' books right across to those which are certainly written with an eye to a market even if they are not deliberately designed and written to the supposed demands of that market. As we have seen, authorship and publishing are extremely chancy occupations and, whilst it is very common for books to fall below expectations in both sales and critical acclaim, it is also not uncommon for books to exceed their expectations and this can happen with general books in the middle range. When such a happy occurrence takes place the publisher can put out extra impressions and can publish (or sell the rights for) a paperback edition for a larger market.

One very good example of a non-fiction book which became an extraordinarily successful bestseller was *The Concise British Flora in Colour* by W. Keble Martin, first published in 1965 by Ebury Press and Michael Joseph and paperbacked by Sphere Books in 1972. This beautiful and scholarly reference book, the result of nearly sixty years' study, found a very large market indeed but in no way could it ever be suggested that the Reverend Keble Martin had spent virtually a lifetime working towards a successful market for a book; his was truly a labour of love which happily became a tremendous popular success.

Another extraordinary bestseller is the more recent *The Country Diary of an Edwardian Lady* by Edith Holden published in facsimile form by Webb & Bower and Michael Joseph in 1977 and a book (if the word is correct) which has been at the top of the hardback bestseller lists longer than any other. This naturalist's diary of 1906, so beautifully printed and bound by the Arnoldo Mondadori company of Italy, is probably the most popular single cultural 'gift book' yet published (as opposed to reference books). It is not a work of specialist scholarship and the facsimile form undoubtedly provides a great proportion of its attraction so that its publishers could clearly hope,[12] as they did, for a reasonable commercial success. That success was greatly helped by the book being selected by a book club, but even so the continued degree of popularity of the book could never have been accurately forecast.[13] Imitators of the *Country Diary* with similar types of books have certainly not had anything like the same success.

So the unpredictability of books makes for difficulty in categorising them according to their market results since markets can surprise even the publishers. However, there are books which are written with a definite eye to a market and it is to these we now turn.

Books for a market

With this category of book we are at the other end of the continuum from the highly specialised scholarly monograph or the serious literary novel. Whereas the author of the monograph or the serious novel is writing virtually for himself (or herself) or at best for a readership that will be known to be limited in size, the author who writes for the market puts the market before his (or her) own interests. At its very worst writing for a market can be pure 'hack' writing for money only, but in the world of books such an over-simplification can be misleading.

If one walks round a large general bookshop and carefully appraises the stock on display it becomes clear quite quickly that there are many types of books which seem to bear a strong similarity to each other. There are, for example, very many cookery books offered for sale, often beautifully illustrated with mouth-watering photographs, but seemingly duplicating each other a great deal in what might be called the area of 'general' cookery. Even though they might not be considered actually to be 'books' the road atlases of Great Britain published for motorists seem (literally) to cover the same ground. Illustrated large-sized general books on the Second World War seem to proliferate. In summer there are hosts of small books or pamphlets giving information on cheap holidays, camping sites, farmhouse accommodation and so on; some of these publications do not even have a named author.

It can therefore be seen that one example of the extreme market-orientated book is where the author disappears altogether and the publishers have decided upon a content which can be put together without actually requiring there to be an author named. My own domestic collection of books includes, for example, a 500-page *AA Road Book of France* with five named contributors but no named editor. The Automobile Association's *Treasures of Britain* lists sixty-five people and organisations to whom the publishers express their gratitude for major contributions, but the only information about the editorship is that the book was 'edited and designed by Drive Publications Limited for the Automobile Association'. Similarly the *AA Book of the Car* was edited by the same subsidiary of the association, though in addition to lists of contributors, artists, designers, photographers, firms and organisations who all contributed (146 in all) a technical editor and a technical adviser are named. The *Reader's Digest Great World Atlas* was planned under the direction of a named 'emeritus professor of geography' and there is a long list of people and organisations who contributed to and advised on this also. The *Reader's Digest Complete Atlas of the British Isles* also lists many people and organisations who made 'major contributions' but the atlas itself is simply described as being 'edited and designed by The Reader's Digest Association, London'.

Atlases, car manuals, road books and the like are specialised types of publications, often offered for sale more by direct mail rather than through conventional retail outlets, but they usefully exemplify the strong market orientation of the book and the relative lack of importance of the author or editor. Editing of such technical manuals is a very demanding and complicated business and the editors must be people of considerable knowledge and skill, but the product itself overshadows its producers and it is significant that so many books-for-a-market of this type are known by the name of the organisation rather than the author (or even by the name of a conventional publisher). Thus the purchasers are conditioned to think of the *AA* Book of the Car, the *Reader's Digest* World Atlas – plus, of course, the *Guinness* Book of Records, the *Good Housekeeping* cookery books, the *Michelin* guides and so on. Even at the scholarly level Oxford University Press have been very successful in establishing their 'brand image' with the *Oxford* dictionaries and *Oxford* companions which have distinguished editors of impeccable qualifications – but the books are still marketed primarily as *Oxford* books.

A rather curious form of marketing occurs in educational publishing when publishers retain the names of original authors for subsequent editions of successful textbooks. *Gray's Anatomy* is perhaps the most famous medical textbook in the world, known by title to thousands of people who have possibly never even seen a copy, certainly never read one. Yet the original author has been dead many years, the current authors (who obviously change with the years) are scholars who continue to edit the work for the modern market and the publishers themselves would be wilful in the extreme to consider changing the title to *Bloggs's Anatomy*. Although the current editors of textbooks in both secondary and higher education may receive both monetary reward and professional acclaim for being the current editors of a well-known text (and to be invited, for example, to become an editor of one of the highest-level law books can be a great honour), nevertheless the books themselves are the important thing and with no market there would be no further edition of the book.

Obviously one must here distinguish between 'scholarly' texts, middle-range texts and what might be referred to derogatorily as 'crammers'. The last of these are the ones most directly aimed at a market, they make no claims to scholarship, only to helping students to pass examinations with the minimum amount of effort. As such their editorships carry no kudos and may even result in a loss of prestige. These are the books which are regarded as 'hack' work because the author/editor must work wholly on content for a market. Sales are the only criteria of success.

Up to this point we have been considering some rather extreme forms of publication which I have known referred to as 'non-books' on the grounds that atlases, car manuals, cookery books and travel guides are all works to which one may turn for reference but they are not books for reading. This is an interesting point of view since it raises a question which will be dealt with in more detail later in this book. It is worth noting, however, at this point where we are considering authorship that, whilst the editor of a dictionary, a companion, a guide or a textbook may well not write the book with a view to it being read from start to finish, it does not necessarily follow that other books which *could* be read from cover to cover necessarily *are* read in this way.

If one looks at many very reasonably priced illustrated hardcover non-fiction books in the general bookshop, departmental store or even tobacconists' and newsagents' shops there are plenty of examples to be seen of those books which are commonly referred to as 'coffee-table' books. The implication is that these are books to be picked up, looked at, leafed through and put down again. The important attraction in such books is the quality of illustration rather than the text, yet the book *does* have an author and obviously the author must have sufficient knowledge of the subject to be able to write knowledgeably and interestingly on the book's special subject.

There are many illustrated books of this sort on subjects such as transport (especially old-style transport), wildlife, various parts of the world, houses, gardens, furniture and so on. Many are published by publishing houses with specialist skills in selecting the right topics, commissioning authors and picture editors and, especially, in mass-marketing the products. The author will normally be commissioned, and such is the international aspect of the publishing enterprise that authors may well be translated from their native language into many other languages, the text, in effect, being built round the basic framework of the pictures. The leading British publisher in this field is undoubtedly Paul Hamlyn who has had tremendous success in publishing and marketing books of this type. It is important to link publishing and marketing together in this particular operation as direct agreements with home retail outlets such as W. H. Smith and now Marks & Spencer (who have begun to publish under their own 'St Michael' imprint) and tremendous skills in export agreements are essential for the success of the books. Looking at two Hamlyn titles on my son's bookshelf, both dealing with transport, it is noteworthy that the spines give the title of the book and the name Paul Hamlyn, but the author's name does not go on the spine.

Coffee-table books and many non-fiction books which it is hoped will reach a mass market are books on themes such as cookery, gardening, do-it-yourself and, recently, slimming. When competition in a particular theme is heavy publishers often try to use special brand names to get the edge on their competitors. Mention has been made of the AA, Good Housekeeping and so on. At a more personal level the publisher can use the name of a person already known, usually in other media, so as to give a special cachet to a book. Today the link-up with television is obviously very useful indeed, though with the growth of the BBC as a book publisher itself the conventional book publishers are often second in the queue. But famous names are certainly popular in areas such as cookery, with authors like Fanny Craddock, Delia Smith and so on. In gardening Percy Thrower is an obvious example. In do-it-yourself there is Geoffrey Burdett. In sport too authors' names can be important and so one finds instruction books on everything from archery to yachting being prepared for the mass market with authors who are popular household names on the cover.

The fact that the person's name is on the cover does not necessarily mean that the author has done all the work himself or herself. Not all cooks, gardeners, athletes and sportsmen are necessarily good teachers or writers so often they need help with their work and this may be provided by the publisher. This can extend from the assistant who does routine collecting of facts which the author uses, right across to the virtual ghosting of the book which the author has given little more to than a name.

The use of authors' names on books which are in varying degrees ghosted extends across to autobiography also. Publishers are always on the look-out for topical themes and especially topical people. So it is by no means uncommon to find a book being published about the person who, for example, stole the Ruritanian crown jewels which is described as 'in collaboration with' or 'assisted by' a professional writer, usually a journalist. Such books can fall within the area of 'instant publishing' which means that the publishers believe there is a sizeable market for the book if it can be got out quickly enough. The famous Israeli military operation at Entebbe was a good example of an event which needed a book to follow very quickly indeed if it was to capitalise on the current interest. Scandals, especially those concerning sex or politics, or even better both together, demand instant books. For this type of publishing the author is simply a person with journalistic narrative skills who can produce a reasonably accurate and interesting account at very high speed. Scholarly analyses are not wanted, nor are authors who need to ponder, draft, consider, redraft and then go back to polish the syntax. Speed is of the essence for a market that may not be there in a few weeks' time. So in this sort of writing the author is really being required to turn out so many thousand words on a given subject for a given deadline. The work is very much akin to journalism in the way that time presses, the content must be dealt with in a craftsmanlike way but the author will gain credit more for 'reporting' skills than for philosophical analyses.

Turning now to fiction the position is difficult to analyse in a way wholly similar to that of non-fiction as fiction authors writing consciously and deliberately for a mass market are not handling factual material but are still working imaginatively in a way similar to that of more serious novelists. By this I do not mean to imply that the mass-market fiction author and the serious literary novelist are very close together in their work but it is essential to recognise that non-fiction material is in many ways simpler to handle than fiction. Thus the sportsman who cannot express himself well in writing can still put over ideas for his ghost writer to transcribe. The pop star who perhaps cannot write at all can still be the 'author' of a ghosted autobiography. But no novelist can be ghosted under any normal circumstances since the form and the content are inseparable. It follows therefore that no matter how commercial and market-orientated certain fiction writing may be the author must have some special ability to *write* a story.

It is often suggested that westerns, romances and certain types of thriller are the most common genres of mass-market fiction. It is doubtful if more than a handful of writers of westerns reach a mass market these days as that particular genre has not the popularity it enjoyed in days past. The writing of thrillers can be a fairly standard type of authorship, with somewhat mechanical plots, stereotyped characters and contrived situations. Sex and violence are usually routine ingredients of such novels at the present time. Romantic fiction, normally regarded as being novels written for a female readership only, is noteworthy for its limited range of plots, its easily recognisable characterisation and its predictably happy endings. (If the ending is unhappy the author is obviously aspiring to higher things.)

Once upon a time, in 1961 actually, Marghanita Laski wrote an essay on the romantic novel which has never yet been bettered.[14] Strangely enough her essay was written to discuss the reasons for the decline in the popularity of romantic fiction. Since then it has, of course, risen steadily in popularity through mass-market sales of paperbacks (which she barely mentions) which came into being after the decline of the commercial libraries (which she does discuss). Miss Laski's analysis of the genre itself is particularly perceptive since she asks if *popular romance, as a kind, is more reasonably regarded as an offshoot from the main stream of fiction, like detective or cowboy stories, or whether it stands at one end of a continuum of English domestic novels whose apex is touched by* Middlemarch. *Or to put it another way, are popular romances read for satisfactions similar to if simpler than those to be derived from* Middlemarch *or for satisfactions so different as to be another kind?*

She accepts that at all sorts of intellectual and aesthetic levels there are people who read 'for the enjoyment of good story-telling and a good story'. The ability to tell a good story is not an attribute only of novelists whose work may be judged as what Miss Laski calls 'finally enriching' and it can be a skill of 'those who provide only escape'. But

an element of escape is present in even the best domestic novels, escape, in this context, being taken as meaning the provision of an imagined world or part of a world pleasanter and more shapely than life and therefore providing a relaxing retreat from it. In this sense even our best domestic novels provide some escape.

and Miss Laski gives examples from the usual nineteenth-century novels but does not discuss those of the mid-twentieth century.

The crux of the matter lies in whether the romantic novelist has some knowledge of life in the social settings which she uses for her story and if 'mistakes are made of probability, of language, of relationship' then these 'must, in all but the simplest readers, destroy credence'. But beyond the knowledge of life and its accurate portrayal is the question as to 'the amount that can be learnt about life, about how to live it oneself and how other people make out'. Miss Laski suggests that in many cases what can be learnt from popular romance can be 'stuck on a pin-point', that the depiction of life is naive, over-simplified and, as a constant diet, can do more harm than good. Her conclusion is that 'no craft can establish standards without informed criticism, and without some standards of criticism no consumer knows how to reject the second-rate and demand the better'. She suggests that both writers and readers are 'entitled to informed and informative criticism' but recognises that criticism on literary pages of this genre is rare and few people are capable of it, so she suggests the BBC (then) Light Programme as the place with 'one of the better romantic novelists' as the person to do the reviewing.

The comments made by Miss Laski on romantic fiction are relevant, with some adaptation, to most types of mass-market fiction and they raise important questions as to what the authors of this type of fiction are writing *for*. It can be argued that they are writing simply for money, which is what many writers of non-fiction, journalists and the like are writing for. If such authors are successful in their writing they *do* make money because there *is* a readership for their books and readers are voluntarily buying the books, normally in paperback format. Since the buyers of the books could spend their money on other consumer goods a choice has been made and the customer has made her decision. If, after reading the book by the particular author she is disappointed by it then she will not buy any further books by that author and the author will cease to make money.

So, at its most commercial level, novel writing in this genre requires the author to give the reader what she wants. The customer is right, not the author. If the plot is trite, the characters cardboard and the action totally implausible and illogical these things do not matter so long as the reader is happy. What Miss Laski regrets is that there is no mediator to tell the readers that they are buying substandard goods. From Miss Laski's viewpoint the customer can well be wrong, very wrong indeed, and needs protecting from herself. Standards must be established by the 'better' novelists if romantic fiction is to be considered to be on the same continuum as *Middlemarch*. If no such standards can be observed then, it would seem, romantic fiction along with westerns and detective stories must be regarded as some sort of cul-de-sac and rather stagnant backwater quite separate from the main stream of 'literature'.

Since Miss Laski's article was published in 1961 the literary criticism of romantic fiction does not seem to have advanced a great deal. The BBC book programmes only discuss it occasionally as a special genre and a romantic novel of the more 'popular' type will rarely be reviewed. Regular reviewing in the ordinary press is not commonplace, though Elizabeth Grey does review it, again as such, in *The Times*. For a time the *Sunday Telegraph* had a monthly short block review devoted to it, but overall romantic fiction novels are still kept apart from conventional novels and reviewing of this genre even such as there is can hardly be considered to be taken seriously in spite of the fact that surveys indicate that this is the most popular form of fiction with women. Clearly the literary 'standard setters' are not very interested.

Yet there are annual prizes for historical and contemporary romantic novels and there is a prize for the best new novelist of the year, all organised through the Romantic Novelists' Association which is the voluntary body set up in 1960 to raise the standards of the writing of romantic fiction. The publishers whose books win the prizes obviously use the fact to try to boost sales, but in general it must be accepted that the RNA prizes carry much less weight than do the more literary ones. The ultimate success of this type of fiction – as with the 'popular' detective stories, thrillers, westerns, adventure stories and mildly pornographic novels – remains measured by the sales figures and authors will acknowledge that royalties form a larger part of their discussions at parties than do literary aspirations.

Yet authors of popular fiction who can write to full novel length of at least 60,000 words are not robots or automata as some people seem to assume. It is often suggested by people with no knowledge of, for example, romantic fiction to authors in that genre that, as the books are so simple in plot and stereotyped in characters, 'anyone' could write them. Actuality is just the reverse. Mills & Boon, the most successful publishers of romantic fiction in the world, receive two or three unsolicited manuscripts every day. They publish fourteen hardback novels a month, ten of which go on to paperback editions with very large print runs. Yet Mills & Boon editors admit that if they can find three or four really good new writers *a year* they count themselves lucky. The ability to write romantic fiction that will satisfy the publisher's editors, who themselves have to judge their readers' tastes, is a rare facility.

Talking to romantic novelists about their work, as I have done on several occasions, it becomes clear that even within this genre there are many differences between authors. Some are almost compulsive writers who can produce a 60,000 word novel each month and would probably continue writing even if their royalties were miniscule, which they are not. Some are women (as there are very few men writers in this genre) who have great difficulty in getting novels published but have a moderate success writing short stories or even 'confessionals' for magazines. Some, particularly authors who have a skill in writing what are known as 'gothic' romances, are published by American houses for their home market but do not find publishers in Britain. In all, the specialist world of romantic fiction is by no means homogeneous and there is even specialism in contemporary romance, historical romance, hospital romance and mystery romance, with most authors restricting themselves to a particular type or period.

Writing for the romance market is most certainly a commercial operation, which no author would deny. The books must sell to readers, so the standards are set by the publisher's editors who must judge for the readers, not by critics. Such is the publication rate of romantic novels that critics would be hard pressed to cope with them all even if they wanted to, but, also, such is the rate of consumption amongst many readers that they too would have no time for reading reviews. The romantic novel bears more similarity to the magazine or the television serial than it does to the one-off novel of the literary genre. Both of these media are regular in their output and it is regularity that romance readers seek. No critics review issues of magazines or the weekly episodes of *Crossroads* or *Coronation Street* but women's magazines and these television serials all have readership and viewers numbered in millions. To write for such magazines or television programmes is to write for an audience and this is what the authors of romantic fiction, thrillers, westerns and all mass-market fiction do.

But whilst being aware of the fact that their writing is to be published for a mass market, the authors cannot actually write for a 'market' as such. It is an uncontested fact amongst authors and publishers in romantic fiction that a woman who decides first that she wants to make some money and then secondly that the romantic novel is a good source of money is virtually certain to fail. No matter how simple the formula may seem to be, few women have the innate ability for this writing and, though it may seem curious, with such 'fairy-story' writing, the author must be *sincere* in what she writes to make a success of it. If the analogy with the fairy story is taken a little further it can be noted that no author really believes in dragons, wicked queens, fair maidens locked in high towers and the like, but with the right ingredients put together so that virtue triumphs and wickedness is punished a very satisfying story can be produced. In many ways romantic fiction is a form of adult fairy story, normally using agreed formulae and conventional ingredients. The skill of the author lies in being able to tell the story in such a way that the reader will suspend disbelief and derive enjoyment from what is basically a simple story skilfully told.

A successful romantic novel will establish both the plot and the principal characters in the first few pages. It will have a heroine with whom the women readers can identify so she must not be too far away from a social status they can understand. There must be a hero who is very masculine and preferably a dominating character. Minor characters may include relatively stereotyped servants, grandmothers and, of course, the 'other woman' who frequently is raven-haired and well-to-do, two attributes which put her beyond redemption! Given such a narrow area in which to write it could be argued that the miracle is how so many authors can continue to find new twists to such a restricted basic theme. Yet romantic novelists never seem to have serious problems of finding new 'plots' and it is therefore reasonable to conclude that they do have a quality of imagination which is creative in this extraordinarily limited yet highly popular field.

Perhaps the fairest assessment of mass-market-orientated fiction is that authors who succeed in this category are people who have an ability to work within narrow confines, who accept the limitations of their work and do not worry too much about the lack of literary kudos, but who can write, and seem to enjoy writing, fairly simple stories for a wide audience whose pure enjoyment of the books is sufficient. If this is a reasonable conclusion to draw then Miss Laski's problem of deciding whether romantic fiction is part of the mainstream of literature or a different branch of the river altogether does not matter terribly. Reviewing by 'one of the better romantic novelists' would be biased because someone has to decide what is meant by 'better' and the criteria Miss Laski would obviously use would be elitist, literary criteria; it would be akin to having the literary editor of the *Sunday Times* seeking a reviewer for *Woman* or *Woman's Own*. Market-orientated fiction lives by its appeal to the many, not to the specialised few, hence its commercial nature and its need to adapt itself to the needs and wants of the reader, who, as the customer, is always right.

This does not mean, though, that the most successful writer of westerns, romances, thrillers or mild pornography will be the author who coldly calculates what the market wants and then tries to construct a book with the right ingredients. Such writers are legion in the would-be romantic novelists who are constantly rejected. The basic ability to *write*, to be able to tell a story, to be able to *communicate* with the reader still marks out the successful authors from the failures. Many a popular romantic novelist or thriller writer can actually *communicate* far better than some highly esteemed literary novelists; the prime difference lies in the content of their communication. Thus, the relationship between author and content, with emphasis on author, marks out the avant-garde (often 'difficult') literary novel and the relationship between content and reader (or market) marks out the mass-market novelist who would probably be happier to be described as a good 'craftsman' or 'craftswoman' than as a literary 'genius'.

This chapter has looked in detail at the problems of authorship of books of all types and has stressed the importance of the creative function of the author. It is apparent though that when the book has been written it must be published and bought by someone if it is to be a means of communication rather than just a dead artefact. The next step in the chain of communication is the complex matter of publishing the book and it is to this we turn in the following chapter.

Chapter 3

PUBLISHING

What is publishing?

Simple dictionary definitions of the word 'publish' usually refer to such things as 'making public', 'announcing' and even 'proclaiming', but when a more direct reference is made to publishing which involves books the dictionary definition will refer to putting forth and offering for sale the work of an author.

It is not uncommon for book publishers to describe themselves in ways which draw upon analogies with midwives in medicine. Publishers often see themselves as intermediaries who help the authors bring their works out into the great big world. This somewhat anatomical analogy, however, is a rather dangerous and misleading one, as midwives are concerned with bringing into the world single children, perhaps twins and, much more rarely, further multiples. The book publisher certainly does help an author to bring his (or her) work to the readers but he (or she) is also fundamentally concerned with the production and dissemination of *multiple* copies of an author's work. If the midwife analogy were taken more closely the publisher would have to be said to be involved in the currently popular concept of 'cloning'.

Whilst it is not actually *wrong* to think of the publisher acting as a middle man between author and reader so far as the book is concerned, publishers also must be recognised as acting for authors so as to take copies of the books to the readers. It is the multiple aspect of the publishers' functions that brings about the important change from *an* author having written *a* book to the publisher producing perhaps thousands of *copies* of a title for perhaps millions of readers.

From a social viewpoint, therefore, the publisher is the person who moves things along from the rather solitary work of the author to the very public aspect of multiple readership. Looked at in this way, rather than focusing on the midwifery aspects of coaxing the title from the author, it can be more clearly appreciated how a publishing house must be made up of a variety of people with very different roles and, amongst this variety, editing is only one.

This point is worth stressing, because so many people (especially young undergraduates with rather vague ideas of becoming 'publishers') seem to think that book publishing consists almost wholly of book editing and they fail to realise that there are other equally important functions to be performed in the long and involved process of changing a manuscript into a print-run of a sellable book.

The business of publishing

Book publishing is a complicated business process which requires both organising and financial skills. In some ways it appears to have a rather beguiling simplicity, which can be exaggerated by accounts of entrepreneurs who began book publishing on a shoe-string and went on to make a great success of their enterprises. Many very well-known publishing houses are surprisingly small in staff numbers and visitors have been known to express considerable surprise at the few people there are in the building which houses the publishing firm.

If one thinks of a 'publisher' as a man or woman who runs a publishing house then there are certain jobs that must be done, but by no means is it necessary for all those jobs to be done in the house itself. In very simple terms, the publisher needs to get hold of manuscripts from authors, read them, perhaps correct and alter them and get them into a state where they can be handed over for making into book form. The first process is done by what we call the editorial department. The agreed manuscript must then be made into a printed book, with a cover, so this involves printing and binding, which uses paper and board as well as printing technology. Most of this work will be sub-contracted to firms of printers and binders, but the publishing house will need someone to look after the process of production.

Once the manuscript has become multiple copies in book form the problem of getting rid of those copies is paramount, so (apart from having to warehouse them anyway) the publisher needs sales people who will try to sell copies to bookshops and other retail or wholesale 'outlets' and advertising and publicity staff who will try to make the appropriate reading public aware of the existence of the book itself. Successful selling of books into bookshops is absolutely basic to the continuance of a publishing house, yet it is rare indeed to find any novel, film or play in which a 'publisher' is depicted as a sales executive.

The simple-looking flow from editorial to production to sale is not, by any means, the whole story of publishing. At every stage of the process the publisher is involved in financial calculations and, inevitably, risks. Publishing which makes profits provides risk capital for the publishing of new books. Publishing which fails to make profits is deprived of risk capital for new books. This simple rule obtains no matter what the type of book may be, unless the publishing house is enabled to run at a loss through some form of external subsidy. As a writer on the publishing of scholarly books in the USA once put it, 'A book that would bankrupt a scholarly publisher does not fall within the proper domain of scholarly publishing.'[1]

At the heart of successful publishing, no matter what type of book may be involved, lies the need for skill in deciding, not only what titles to publish by what authors, but also how many copies of a book to publish at what price. This statement is quite basic to publishing and yet is frequently not appreciated by book con-sumers. A low print-run means a high unit cost per book; a high print-run enables a low unit cost to be attained. Popular fiction in paperback form is often quite cheap to buy. The cheapness however is not primarily because the book is a paperback, it is because the book has been printed to the tune of perhaps hundreds of thousands of copies. Once this essential basis of print-runs and prices is understood it can be further seen why some slim specialist scholarly books in, say, medicine or history seem to be rather expensive and why quite a fat paperback edition of a standard student textbook seems relatively cheap.

There are, of course, all sorts of other considerations which come into play in determining the income which a publisher might obtain from a book. The sale of foreign rights, both in the English language and in foreign languages, can be very important sources of revenue. Sales of copies to book clubs, who then sell directly to their members, can be very useful, and an agreement before publication with a book club which will take x thousand copies clearly will reduce the initial unit costs of publication. The sale of other rights – perhaps to newspapers or magazines for extracts or serialisation – may produce both direct income and also more interest in a book. Television or film versions of a book can again provide direct revenue and considerable stimulation to sales. One has only to look around in bookshops to see how many paperbacks on show have film or TV links. Some bookshops even have special racks for such books headed 'TV or Film Tie-ins'.

If one appreciates how many different forms of revenue may be contributing to a publisher's income it must then be more apparent how important it is for the publisher to 'sell' the book in various ways. When one also considers that the whole of the British book trade in 1980 published a grand total of 48,158 books of which 36,092 were completely new titles in the one year (that is, excluding reprints, new editions and translations) then the astonishing complexity of the book publishing industry may be better appreciated.

The organisation of publishing

Since book publishing houses can vary in size and complexity from the publisher who literally operates from his (or her) own living-room right the way across to a multinational corporation it is impossible to describe one simple structure which would apply to all forms of publishing. Nevertheless, from what has already been said, it can be seen that there are certain functions and certain lines of action which are very general to all book publishing.

In the beginning is the author, but authors may seek publishers themselves, may use literary agents to approach publishers for them or, in quite a number of instances, may actually be sought out by publishers themselves.

Within the publishing house itself there will be editorial staff of varying grades including the active seekers of authors and positive creators of books, often referred to as commissioning editors, as well as desk editors who are more concerned with the minutiae of the manuscripts themselves. There will be people preparing the copy for the printers and there will be production staff seeing to it that printers and binders actually fabricate the books. Production staff will be concerned with the costs of production, as will the sales and marketing staff whose job it is, to put the matter very basically, to get rid of the books.

Sales staff will include publishers' representatives, whose work takes them to wholesalers and retailers 'selling in' the books before actual publication. Marketing and publicity staff will also work on advertising the books wherever seems most appropriate within cost limits and in trying to ensure that people who do want the books in their shops can actually get copies within a reasonable period of time.

Sales of books may be made to a variety of different buyers, which can include wholesalers as well as retailers, library suppliers, school contractors, book clubs and other direct mail operators. The sale of subsidiary rights is also a further important source of income. British publishers overall export about 40 per cent of their trade, so export sales also are vital to a house's success.

In all the activities which take place money flows in or out of the house. Authors must be paid advances and royalties. All books sold must be invoiced and discounts of various sorts allowed. So complicated is the discounting system in the book trade that a separate handbook is needed for reference purposes. Every publishing house must have a competent accounts department and there is also a need, as a house gets larger, for positive financial planning for new ventures.

In the most general terms, therefore, it could be said that even if a publishing 'house' originally consisted of the one entrepreneur, he (or she) would have to cope with editorial, production, sales and marketing, publicity, rights and finance. Some of these functions could be sub-contracted; printing and binding usually is. A small house might have its list 'represented' by the representatives of a larger house or an independent firm of book representatives. But whatever the organisation might look like in staff the basic functions must be performed.

The variety of publishing

A dictionary definition of a 'book' is of very little help in furthering an understanding of book publishing. Most of us can agree, in a general way, that we know what a book looks like, though we might have a little difficulty in deciding between a slim paperback book and a rather fat pamphlet. On the whole, though, we recognise a book, usually, by it being a printed document with a reasonably substantial cover, securely (we hope) bound, and sold to us through a recognised retail outlet. A UNESCO definition of a book, adopted in 1964, defines it simply as 'a non-periodical printed publication of at least 49 pages exclusive of the cover pages' which helps to distinguish it from booklets, journals or pamphlets, but is nevertheless a very broad sort of definition which many publishers might find difficult to apply.[2]

Book publishers themselves are more difficult to categorise as they vary enormously. Twice a year the *Bookseller*, the trade journal of the British book trade, issues lists of 'Book Publishers' Output' over the past six months, based upon the weekly publication lists which are a feature of every issue of the journal. If a publication has been given an International Standard Book Number (ISBN) then it will be included in the list under its publisher. The full list printed between pages 428 and 454 of the

Bookseller of 7 February 1981 lists approximately 2,400 different publishers, alphabetically from 'A & W Publishers, USA'
with one new edition to 'Zwemmer' with two new books. The
range of new titles published is from 863 publishers with one new
book to Academic Press, Hale, Oxford University Press and
Wiley all with more than 300 new titles each (leaving aside new
editions) with OUP at the top of the list with 369 new titles.

Roughly speaking one-third of the book publishers listed in the
Bookseller's half-yearly report had published only one new book
each in those six months. An analysis of the previous half-year,
January to June 1980, gave 752 publishers out of approximately
2,200 listed with only one new book – again, roughly one-third.
These figures must indicate that book publishing is extremely
diffused in this country if each half-year can result in listings of
over 2,000 book publishers. But as the editor of the *Bookseller*
explained, 'The figures cover the title output of organisations and
individuals in this country who publish books, and the output of
overseas publishers whose books are available in this country
from a sole agent who holds stock.'[3] Thus, the figure of 347 new
titles from Academic Press does not necessarily mean that
Academic Press, *London*, published all those new titles.
Academic Press is part of a large international publishing house,
so many of those titles could be published abroad (say in the USA)
and held in stock in London. Also we must note that the title
output includes 'individuals' who publish books as well as
'organisations' and organisations can include bodies whose
primary activity is not book publishing. Such names as 'Mason,
P. J.', 'Morro, N. Y.' and 'Thornton, J.' might well be individuals
who each published one new book and no new editions between
July and December 1980. Even more interestingly, 'Mason, P. J.'
published one book at 70 pence, whilst the books from the other
two publishers cost £4.95 and £5.00 respectively.

Organisations whose primary aim in life is an activity other
than book publishing would include the Midland Counties
Rugby Football Union (one new book at £1), the American Bar
Association (one new book at £10.50) and the Association of
British Wild Animal Keepers (one new book at £1.40).

Without doubt, book publishing is done by a very heter-
ogeneous collection of people and organisations and, as the
editor of the *Bookseller* points out, 'The bookselling side of the
trade has to deal – in greater or lesser degree – with *all* the
output.'[4] Certainly if a book is published and has a price attached
to it, then it must be assumed that the publishers are hoping that
someone will buy it.

Nevertheless, although it is useful to remind ourselves that
book publishing is not restricted to any special types of individuals or organisations, and anyone in Britain is free to publish a
book if he wants to, it is wise to note that the Price Commission in
its 1978 report on the book trade said that there were 'at least
1,700 publishers in the UK with a total home and export turnover
of some £400 million in 1976; these include 350 members of the
Publishers' Association whose turnover represents about 85 per
cent of the annual total.' The commission further noted that '44
large companies' accounted for about 60 per cent of the total
turnover.[5]

The Publishers' Association itself, in a small book (sixty-two
pages and therefore a book by UNESCO's definition) published
in 1977, said that at the time of publication, 'There are more than
4,000 entries in Whitaker's "UK Publishers and their Addres-
ses". They include private societies, associations and institutions
which publish reports, local guides and booklets from time to
time but are not regularly engaged in the business of book
publishing. The members of the Publishers' Association, about
400 companies, account for at least 90 per cent of the national
turnover (revenue from sales).'[6] There was a further statement
that in 1975 turnover was £351 million and 41 per cent of this
was attributable to export.

Both these extracts draw our attention to the great variety of
publishers and publications to be found in Britain and make it
impossible for anyone to be dogmatic about what a 'publisher' is.
From the point of view of book publishing as a business then
obviously the restricted membership of the Publishers' Association is the more realistic, though even so membership of the PA
only requires that a firm should be 'carrying on in the United

Kingdom the business of bona fide book publishers', which is not asking a great deal of a genuine publishing house. From the viewpoint of the book reader though, whether buyer or borrower, there is no doubt that a very broad viewpoint needs to be taken. If, for example, a scientist wishes to obtain a copy of a highly specialised publication which is essential to his (or her) work he is not interested in who has published it, or how it is being sold and distributed, so long as he can obtain a copy as quickly as possible. Unfortunately for the reader he may find that the publisher of this book is a specialist research organisation first and publisher only in a very minor way and so the distribution and marketing of the book is not handled in a very professional way. As a result the would-be reader may not be able to obtain the book easily through conventional 'trade' channels, such as ordinary bookshops, and direct mail purchase by reader from publisher may be the easiest way to obtain the book. With an estimated 300,000 'titles' in print it is clear that no bookshop can hope to stock more than a tiny fraction of those titles and so the very breadth of publishing is, seen this way, too much for the shop-based book selling system.

Clive Bingley has argued cogently that[7]

It is now coming to be acknowledged . . . that different categories of books require to be marketed in different ways. . . . What is needed is a realisation that 'books' are no longer a single uniform commodity, but that the term is a collective one for a wide range of very disparate commodities which require a very different set of approaches to their marketing, according to their natures.

Types of books and publishing

Book publishing is such a broad activity that it is inevitable that successful publishing necessitates some specialisation. Very large firms may have sections devoted to, say, adult fiction, children's books and reference works, but no one house could hope to publish every type of book written.

The classification of books themselves is a difficult and contentious business, as any publisher, bookseller or librarian well knows. All classification is, in the final analysis, an arbitrary affair. Libraries and bookshops normally use a basic division between fiction and non-fiction in their display of books, though if the Dewey decimal system is strictly applied in a library fiction can be classified as a part of the literature of the particular language.

In publishing itself there is little use made of the all-encompassing schemes such as Dewey or the Library of Congress, but in Britain J. Whitaker & Sons classify all books as they are published at first on a weekly basis and eventually these are cumulated on a monthly, quarterly and annual basis for *Whitaker's Cumulative Book List*. When Whitaker's statistical tables are published in the *Bookseller* the books published are classified under forty-six different headings from, alphabetically, Aeronautics to Wireless and Television. Some categories are fairly small; for example, the smallest for the year 1980 was 'general science' with only 104 titles (including reprints, new editions, translations and limited editions). By contrast the really big categories could contain several thousands, with 'fiction' leading the field in 1980 with 5,145 titles overall.

Table 3.1 gives details of the completely new titles (excluding reprints, etc.) published in nineteen selected categories during 1978, 1979 and 1980. The categories were selected by the *Bookseller* itself to illustrate the growth from 1979 to 1980 in titles and it can therefore be safely assumed that these categories are a good representative selection of the whole range. As Table 3.1 shows, for the nineteen selected categories of books, nearly all of them have shown increases in title output between 1978 and 1979 and between 1979 and 1980. In some cases, such as the categories of 'commerce', 'industry' and 'religion', the increase between 1978 and 1980 has been over two-thirds. No category listed had a decrease between 1978 and 1980, though there were six cases of decrease in one year or the other.

The details for the totals of 'all titles', which includes also the other twenty-seven categories not used as examples in Table 3.1, show an increase of 11 per cent from 1978 to 1979, 15 per cent from 1979 to 1980 and a two-year increase from 1978 to 1980 of 28 per cent, which is a considerable increase in *title* output at a time when the book trade is suffering from both the general problems of declining sales because of the recession and also export problems because of the 'strong' pound.

Table 3.1
NEW TITLES PUBLISHED IN THE UK, 1978 TO 1980

Category	1978 Number	1979 Number	% increase 1978–79	1980 Number	% increase 1979–80	% increase 1978–80
Art	1,016	999	−2	1,164	+17	15
Biography	847	834	−2	939	+13	11
Chemistry and physics	578	562	−3	647	+15	12
Children's books	2,324	2,587	+11	2,765	+7	19
Commerce	611	813	+33	1,061	+31	74
Education	772	846	+10	1,047	+24	36
Engineering	883	1,059	+20	1,187	+12	34
Fiction	2,602	2,687	+3	2,900	+8	11
History	955	1,048	+10	1,178	+12	23
Industry	313	366	+17	541	+48	73
Law and public administration	837	1,012	+21	1,191	+18	42
Literature	759	870	+15	862	−1	14
Medical science	1,796	2,072	+15	2,663	+29	48
Natural sciences	893	961	+8	1,079	+12	21
Political science and economy	2,162	2,626	+21	3,171	+21	47
Religion	779	930	+19	1,293	+39	66
School textbooks	1,565	1,734	+11	1,955	+13	25
Sociology	791	788	−0.4	997	+27	26
Travel and guidebooks	401	428	+7	419	−2	4
All titles	28,285	31,480	+11	36,092	+15	28

Notes

1 The figures are taken from the *Bookseller*, as are the categories used.
2 Figures relate to new titles only. Reprints, new editions, etc., are excluded.
3 Percentages are rounded off to the nearest whole number.

Title output

Some people in the book trade have expressed doubts about the meaningfulness of these title output figures which, overall, give indications of considerable growth in the output of books (as titles) year by year.[8] Table 3.2 shows the growth in new titles and reprints, etc., over a period of twenty-one years. As Table 3.2

Table 3.2

BOOKS PUBLISHED IN THE UK, 1960 TO 1980

Year	New titles*	New editions and reprints	Total	% increase or decrease on previous year
1960	18,794	4,989	23,783	
1961	18,487	6,406	24,853	+4.5
1962	18,975	6,104	25,079	+0.9
1963	20,367	5,656	26,023	+3.8
1964	20,894	5,260	26,154	+0.5
1965	21,045	5,313	26,358	+0.8
1966	22,964	5,919	28,883	+9.6
1967	22,559	7,060	29,619	+2.5
1968	22,642	8,778	31,420	+6.1
1969	23,287	9,106	32,393	+3.1
1970	23,512	9,977	33,489	+3.4
1971	23,563	8,975	32,538	−2.8
1972	24,654	8,486	33,140	+1.8
1973	25,698	9,556	32,254	−2.7
1974	24,342	7,852	32,194	−0.2
1975	27,247	8,361	35,608	+10.6
1976	26,207	8,227	34,434	−3.3
1977	27,684	8,638	36,322	+5.5
1978	29,530	9,236	38,766	+6.7
1979	32,854	9,086	41,940	+8.2
1980	37,382	10,776	48,158	+14.8

*Note: In this table 'New titles' include a small number of translations and limited editions, as the *Bookseller* historical statistics from which these tables are drawn give only two categories for books, 'total' and 'reprints and new editions'.

shows very clearly the increase in title output over twenty years has been quite remarkable, and the large increase in title output in 1980 over the previous year results in a doubling of title output between 1960 and 1980, as well as a spectacular rise from the 34,434 titles of 1976 to 48,158 in 1980, which is virtually 40 per cent in only five years.

Table 3.3

TOTAL BOOKS PUBLISHED BY TEN PUBLISHERS

Publisher	1969	1974	% increase 1969–74	1979	% increase 1974–9	1980	% increase 1979–80
Blackwell Scientific	53	35	−34	61	+74	97	+59
Cape	148	106	−28	89	−16	81	−9
Collins	463	714	+54	460	−36	451	−2
Constable	47	58	+23	44	−24	54	+23
Deutsch	91	95	+4	98	+3	97	−1
Faber & Faber	329	205	−38	199	−3	164	−15
Michael Joseph	106	105	−1	89	−15	90	+1
Oxford University Press	787	591	−25	721	+22	972	+35
Routledge & Kegan Paul	319	208	−35	269	+29	278	+3
Thames & Hudson	139	124	−11	126	+2	135	+7
All publishers in *Bookseller*	32,393	32,194	−1	41,940	+30	48,158	+15

Yet when the *Bookseller* looked at the 1980 title output and found an overall increase of 14.8 per cent from 1979 to 1980 it did not find this mirrored in the individual statistics for ten selected publishing houses, all members of the Publishers' Association and all very well–known houses in the trade. The *Bookseller* table[9] gave details for the years 1969, 1974, 1979 and 1980 for the ten houses and Table 3.3 uses those data rearranged and with percentages calculated. As Table 3.3 shows, the overall differences between 1969–74, 1974–9 and 1979–80 were −1 per cent, +30 per cent and +15 per cent for all the many publishers listed in the *Bookseller* taken together. Certainly the 1969–74 comparison seems to indicate a decline, with seven of the ten publishers showing decreases, and Blackwell Scientific, Faber and Routledge each down more than 30 per cent. But of the three publishers with increases Collins were up in titles published by 54 per cent and Constable were up 23 per cent.

Between 1947 and 1979 all publishers taken together showed an increase of 30 per cent. Half the ten selected publishers showed increases, with Blackwell up 74 per cent, but half were down and this time Collins were down 36 per cent.

For the one-year comparison between 1979 and 1980 all publishers were up, this time by 15 per cent, and six of the ten named publishers were up, Blackwell by 59 per cent and Oxford University Press by 35 per cent. Cape had the biggest decline, but this was only 9 per cent. If we look at the individual publishers for the four selected years it is difficult to find a coherent pattern in the numbers of titles published. If we try to argue that 1969 was a 'boom' time and 1974 was a time of depression then an overall decrease of 1 per cent in title output is surely very small. But of the seven publishers with fewer titles only Michael Joseph was at the figure of 1 per cent – the rest were down 34, 28, 38, 25, 35 and 11 per cent. If the ten publishers are accepted as being indicative of 'trade' publishers, then obviously the trade was, generally speaking, having rather a poor time in 1974 (though Collins and Constable seemed to be expanding their lists nicely).

Looking across to 1979 and 1980 it would seem as if Blackwell Scientific and Oxford University Press were both expanding considerably, whilst Cape and Faber were declining somewhat. Collins's monster output of 714 titles in 1974 looks to be a rather unusual deviation from a more normal output of about 450 titles a year. Deutsch and Thames & Hudson both seem to have a very steady pattern, publishing respectively about 95 and 130 titles a year.

The only reasonable conclusion which can be drawn from these statistics is that title output can vary quite considerably from one year to another and that individual publishers can themselves differ greatly from the overall trend. This, surely, arises from the very broad definitions of both 'books' and 'publishers' used for the compilation of these statistics. Whilst publications from 'one-a-year' publishers are included, and whilst 'publishers' include individuals and organisations which are so transparently not real book publishers it is impossible to say what is happening in the book trade year by year from title output alone.

Publishing and money

Statistics about title output in book publishing are of some value in understanding the enormous variety to be found in this trade but information about titles alone is of very limited use unless one knows how many copies of each title are printed and actually sold. Here, unfortunately, there is no regular source of impartial and reliable information.

Not surprisingly, since book publishing is a highly competitive business, publishers regard print-runs and title sales as very confidential data. Publishers are sometimes willing to make public details of print-runs of books before publication so as to show to the book trade that a new title is expected to be a success. This, it is hoped, will help 'sell in' a title to the retailers and wholesalers. If a book is successful then the publisher does not mind people knowing that sales have been particularly good and perhaps that reprints have been needed.

But it would be a very unusual publisher who was eager to tell the world that the print-run for Mr X's latest thriller or Miss Y's latest literary novel was smaller than for his or her previous book. The publishing world thrives on gossip and speculation and publishers strive hard to give a public appearance of doing well whilst doing their best to conceal any failures. It must also be borne in mind that the *overall* success or otherwise of a publishing house is made up of a large number of small items. As Table 3.3 showed, publishing houses produce quite considerable numbers of what other manufacturers might call 'new lines' each year. When one notes that, for example, Collins published 339 new books and 112 new editions of older books in 1980, in addition to having for sale a whole backlist of titles already published and still in print, then it is clear that Collins derive their income from a vast array of books, some of which will have had large print-runs, some of which will have had small ones, some of which will have made profits and some of which will have probably made a loss.

Publishing is, in many ways, a numbers game and no one could be unimpressed by the extraordinary success of a book such as *The Country Diary of an Edwardian Lady* which was in the hardback bestseller lists for virtually three years. A book such as that is, however, very unusual – though obviously a happy exception for its publishers, Webb & Bower/Michael Joseph. For the most part, with the thousands of new titles published each year a book is hoped to make a contribution to the publisher's revenue at its appropriate level. So the number of copies printed must be gauged against the potential market.

It may, to the casual reader, seem that popular paperback titles are to be seen wherever one turns, so surely these must be very profitable compared to, say, a basic textbook on nursing which is perhaps only sold in one bookshop in the town and is never seen in a department store or newsagent's shop. Yet the popular paperback novel may be seen all around the town because it had a large print-run and is not selling at all well, whereas the nurses' textbook is, and has for years been, a most important regular source of income to its publisher because it sells year after year, new edition after old, at the right price to provide a steady profit.

Tempting though it is to quote the tremendous successes of outstandingly popular authors such as Harold Robbins, James Herriot, Catherine Cookson and a relatively small number of other household names (to book readers), the paperback shelves in many retail outlets are stocked with books which, in spite of their print-runs, may or may not be a financial success.

On the other hand, if we look at academic or scientific publishing we may find monographs on highly specialised subjects which have print-runs of only 2,000 copies or less, which seem to be very highly priced, but because there is a known and carefully calculated market for them can produce a useful profit for the publisher. Multiply the individual monograph by *x* times a year, add on some basic textbooks that have been 'bestsellers' for years, perhaps add on too a few scholarly journals which are well subscribed and the result is a flourishing publishing house.

Financial statistics

Until fairly recent years the book trade was rather notorious for its lack of statistics, but since the 1970s it has become more statistics conscious and both the Publishers' Association and the Booksellers' Association now collect statistics regularly from surveys of their own members as well as disseminating officially collected statistics to their members.

The principal source of official financial statistics about the book trade is *Business Monitor* PQ 489 published by the Business Statistics Office which gives quarterly figures of the UK publishing industry's turnover by book categories, by hardback and paperback and by home and export. The actual sales figures in sterling are recorded and an index of change (based on 1972 as 100) is given for both current (i.e. real) prices and constant (i.e. allowing for inflation) prices.

With so many details contained in the *Business Monitor* figures it is possible for publishers of various sorts of books to work out how their own type of book is doing, quarter by quarter, both in home sales and exports. Such are the varieties of books published that it is only sensible, when trying to take an overall view of the finances of publishing, to note that one area of publishing could well be doing rather badly whilst another one was still flourishing.

If we put aside a special category in the *Business Monitor* of 'publishers' receipts from royalties' the total turnover for the UK publishing industry for 1979 was:

Home sales	£355,512,000
Export sales	£205,981,000
Total sales	£561,493,000

78

Thus export sales accounted for 36.7 per cent of all sales in that year.

The inclusion of publishers' receipts from royalties increases the turnover by about £9.5 million in both home and export, and produces a gross total of:

Home	£365,047,000
Export	£215,333,000
Total	£580,380,000

which gives export a proportion of 37.1 per cent.

However, the above figures are based on actual returns from publishers, and not every company in publishing does contribute to the *Business Monitor* statistics. The coverage of the *Monitor* is officially stated to be 'establishments in the UK employing twenty-five or more persons classified to minimum list heading 489', so that very small publishers would be excluded from the data collection. However, not every publishing firm replies to the requests for information and, as the *Monitor* for the third quarter of 1980 said, response was '71 per cent in terms of the total employment of establishments contributing to the survey'. To allow for the non-response 'estimates of sales, based on their previous returns and the trends noted from responding establishments, have been made for establishments which have failed to respond by the time these results were compiled.'[10] It must, therefore, be noted that the figures given for sales in the *Monitor* tables are partly derived from estimates – in the quarter being used here the figures for 29 per cent of the establishments who were non-respondents not being based on actuality, which means that quite a lot of the *Monitor* finances are derived from careful guesswork – but guesswork just the same.

Also given in the *Monitor* is a figure for what is called 'grossed-up estimates' which are

of the total sales of ALL establishments classified to the minimum list heading 489. This has been obtained by applying to the total sales of the establishments contributing to the inquiry a factor which takes account of the establishments below the employment threshold operated in this inquiry and those establishments, in scope, which have still to make a return. In the calculation of this factor it is assumed that the sales per head of the non-contributing establishments are the same as those of the smaller establishments contributing to this inquiry. The factor used for the current quarter (third quarter of 1980) is 1.453. This factor is only appropriate for the estimation of total sales of all establishments and should not be applied to commodity sales and other figures.

All this means, of course, that the Business Statistics Office is, quite rightly, warning us in the use of the *Monitor* that the figures given do not cover every single publishing house in the country, that small employers are left out, and that of the other publishers approached for information between a quarter and a third either do not reply or reply too late for the analysis. So, even the basic tables have to rely on some estimation, and the 'grossed-up' figures rely upon an even greater amount of estimation.

With these firm caveats in mind, we can now look at the details contained in the *Monitors*, which are most interesting. The total sales, home and export, hardback and paperback, of the categories of books analysed were, for 1979, as shown in Table 3.4. The table excludes publishers' receipts from royalties, which were £18,887,000 in 1979.

Applying a factor of 1.441 for 1979 to give the grossed-up estimates the total grossed-up turnover figure for the year was

Table 3.4

UK PUBLISHING TURNOVER 1979: MAJOR CATEGORIES IN £000s

Bibles (hardback)	8,827
School textbooks	92,899
Technical and scientific	94,180
Fiction, literature & classics	128,992
Children's books	51,276
Other (including paperback bibles)	185,318
Total	561,492

£838,328,000. Of this a grossed-up total of £528,033,000 (63 per cent) was home sales and £310,295,000 (37 per cent) was export sales.

Full details of all the categories of books given in the *Monitor* include both paperback and hardback as well as home and export sales, and Table 3.5 gives both the sums of money involved and the percentages. The table can be used to see what proportion of the total publishing turnover is made up by any category of books, home or export and hardback or paperback.

Table 3.5

UK TURNOVER 1979: ALL CATEGORIES (IN £000s)

	Home	%	Export	%	Total	%
Bibles (H)	3,957	0.70	4,870	0.86	8,827	1.57
School textbooks (H)	22,130	3.9	14,949	2.67	37.079	6.60
School textbooks (P)	29,606	5.27	26,214	4.67	55,820	9.94
Technical & scientific (H)	42,555	7.58	30,609	5.45	73,164	13.03
Technical & scientific (P)	11,877	2.12	9,139	1.63	21,016	3.74
Fiction, literature & classics (H)	47,945	8.54	11,880	2.12	59,825	10.66
Fiction, literature & classics (P)	45,408	8.09	23,759	4.23	69,167	12.32
Children's (H)	28,007	4.99	8,586	1.53	36,593	6.52
Children's (P)	10,560	1.88	4,123	0.73	14,683	2.61
Other (H)	108,667	19.4	38,093	6.78	146,760	26.14
Other (incl bibles) (P)	27,595	4.91	10,963	1.95	38.558	6.87
Total	378,307	67.4	183,185	32.6	561,492	100

It is unfortunate that the category 'other' contributes, in all, virtually a third of the total turnover, which is a very high proportion of the whole for what might be called a 'residual' category. What is even less helpful is the allocation to bibles alone of one category out of only five when hardback bibles represent only 1.57 per cent of the whole turnover and paperback bibles are included in the category of Other (P), which must surely indicate that they are a negligible quantity.

The *Bookseller* categories are forty-six in all and it is a great pity that they and the five *Business Monitor* categories bear so little relationship to each other. For example, in 1979, the second largest title category in the *Bookseller* annual analysis of titles published was 'political science and economy' with 3,364 titles in all, second only to 'fiction' with 4,551. Yet, in the *Business Monitor* tables there is no way of knowing what financial turnover political science and economy achieved.

However, accepting the limitations of the *Business Monitor* statistics there is still considerable value to be gained from being able to see the turnover for the four categories, home, export, hardback and paperback, for a particular category.

For example, there are higher home sales from paperback editions of school textbooks than there are from the hardback editions and this is even more pronounced in the export market. Exports of school texts seem to do well, with a total contribution of 7.34 per cent to total turnover compared to 9.21 per cent from the home sales. By contrast, technical and scientific books, both home and export, sell much more in hardback, but again the export figures are good, making up 7.08 per cent of all turnover compared to the home figure of 9.70 per cent.

Fiction, literature and classics is different yet again, with lower export figures – only 6.35 per cent of overall turnover compared to the home figure of 16.63 per cent. Also fiction sales of hardback and paperback are almost equal to each other on the home market, but in the export market the paperback to hardback ratio is almost two to one.

The market for children's books is much greater at home (6.87 per cent of turnover) than abroad, where it is only 2.26 per cent of all turnover. At home the sales ratio between hardback and paperback is roughly 5:2, but in the export market it is nearer 2:1.

Looking at the export sales overall, we find that the contributions from the named categories are as follows (in percentages):

Bibles (H)	0.86
School textbooks	7.34
Technical & scientific	7.08
Fiction, etc.	6.35
Children's	2.26
All others	8.73
Total export	32.62

Export sales by categories

Even allowing for the vagueness of the 'others' category the above distribution surely indicates a satisfying variety of exports of different sorts of books by British publishers. 'Grossed-up' estimates, being based on a multiplying factor which attempts to take account of both non-respondents and firms too small to be included in the *Monitor* inquiries, must be very general and it is, not surprisingly, impossible to give these for detailed book categories.

Table 3.6

GROSSED-UP ESTIMATES
UK TURNOVER 1974–79 (IN £000s)

Year	Home	Export	Total
1974	221,009	162,686	383,695
1975	279,190	189,909	469,099
1976	320,879	242,575	563,454
1977	368,122	285,262	653,383
1978	445,576	304,754	750,331
1979	526,033	310,295	836,328
1979 un-grossed	378,307	183,185	561,492

From 1974 on the *Business Monitor* has given home and export figures for this calculation and these are shown in Table 3.6. As this table shows, the grossed-up estimate adds a considerable sum of money to the total turnover, as expected from using a multiplier of 1.441. However, since this is really just a multiplication sum to try to estimate the complete amount of turnover achieved in the year it must be remembered that a considerable amount of the money involved is estimated, and, of course, no categorical details can be safely given from these data.

Trends in book sales

The detailed analysis of the figures of turnover for 1979 give only a cross-sectional analysis of one year's trading. Trends in turnover are important and fortunately the *Business Monitor* statistics give quarterly data which can be cumulated for annual comparisons. The Publishers' Association's own *Quarterly Statistical Bulletin*, begun in June 1980, is now doing a fine job of putting together long-term trends, which, using the index of change based on 100 in 1972, enables the book trade to see how each *Business Monitor* category has risen and/or declined since 1972 both at 'current prices' and at 'constant prices' which take account of the effects of inflation.

If we compare the various book categories with each other for constant prices, then the picture is as shown in Table 3.7. This table is limited to one year only, 1979, which is clearly only one year in a trend from 1972. It would be very cumbersome in a book to attempt to reproduce the complete PA chart showing each year between 1972 and 1979, but it can be said in explanation that few categories show any extraordinary index for 1979 which does not seem at least partly explained by trends in previous years. The index figure for bibles (H) for export in 1979 stands at only 46.3, down from 65.6 in 1978, but it is clear that this category of book has not been doing well in recent years. Hardback school textbooks have been falling in real-term sales, whilst paperback editions have been doing better, both in home

Table 3.7

UK TURNOVER 1979: INDEX OF CHANGE FOR CONSTANT PRICES (1972=100)

	Home	Export	Total
Bibles (H)	97.1	46.3	60.4
School textbooks (H)	76.5	84.0	79.3
School textbooks (P)	109.3	125.7	116.5
Technical & scientific (H)	72.4	62.6	68.0
Technical & scientific (P)	103.5	138.6	116.3
Fiction, literature & classics (H)	101.8	56.3	87.7
Fiction, literature & classics (P)	120.6	112.6	117.7
Children's (H)	77.3	73.9	76.5
Children's (P)	84.2	123.0	92.3
Other (H)	138.9	124.5	134.9
Other (incl. bibles) (P)	93.3	180.2	108.1
Publishers' receipts from royalties	109.2	108.0	108.6
Total	103.3	91.9	98.9

and export markets. The picture is fairly similar for technical and scientific books and also for fiction. The home market for children's books has been declining in both formats, as has the export market for hardbacks since 1976, but export of children's paperback books went up 37.2 points in 1973, then to 158.8 in 1974 and after a decline to 1978 at 107.8, picked up to 123.0 in 1979.

The publishers of 'other' books in hardback have had a good set of years since 1972 with a distinct boom in the past two years, though paperbacks have declined a little since a peak of 141.2 in 1977.

One has only to look at the variations of index numbers demonstrated in Table 3.7 to realise that the book trade is a mixed bag of ups and downs, even within one broad category of publishing. Apart from the unfortunately vague 'other' category in hardback which has the highest index figure of all (134.9) in

1979, all the others show the hardback books well below the base line of 100 and, overall, children's paperbacks are down below 100 too, though they are at 123.0 for export.

In fact, the 1979 index figures in general show a strong contrast between the hardback and paperback turnovers, with the hardback market being, almost everywhere, down and the paperback market up. There is too, usually, a favourable index for the export paperback turnover compared to the home market paperback turnover. Yet, with all the variations that there are between categories, taken all together the final index figure for everything is at 98.9, only 1.1 points down on 1972 and this figure has not gone above 107.7 or below 97.1 since the base year of 1972.

In general, therefore, a reasonable conclusion to draw from the analysis of the index figures is that book publishing as a whole has been relatively static in real terms over the period 1972–9, though the home market generally has usually been rather more depressed than the export market, but overall figures tend to mask some fairly considerable variations within and between the categories used in the *Monitor*.

The present state of book publishing

Writing, as this author is for this chapter, in March 1981, just after a particularly unpopular budget which was designed to try to counter some of Britain's major economic problems, it is tempting providence to say just what is the current position of book publishing and what future trends are likely to be.

The book publishing business is, as I have tried to show in this chapter, one of great variety both in the types of books published and in the types of publishers themselves. Much of the statistical data available on publishing is less than satisfactory because the definitions of 'book' and 'publisher' are so broad.

The Publishers' Association itself is now trying to rectify some of these faults by compiling financial data for home and export sales for five major categories of books which are more relevant to their own interests. These cover school publications, university and professional publications, mass-market paperbacks, specialised (largely reference) books and general (including children's) books. Each major category has several subsections. As figures for these sales accumulate the publishing trade will gradually develop a better picture of itself and its trends, but as the scheme only began with the third quarter of 1978 the trend is not yet long-term enough to tell very much. Nevertheless the Publishers' Association *Quarterly Statistical Bulletin* analysis of contributing publishers' sales figures will undoubtedly develop into a vital source of information for the trade so long as publishers continue to supply the necessary data. Even so, the third issue of the *Bulletin* (December 1980) mentions that for the first quarters of 1979 and 1980 sixty-one companies reported in both periods, which obviously does not cover the whole of the book publishing industry.

With all the problems that arise then from restricted information, is it possible to say what has happened, what is happening and what is likely to happen in book publishing? Publishers can be very secretive people when it comes to telling the world about the way things are. In some ways they have reputations not unlike farmers' – both groups seem to enjoy telling people how badly they are doing, even when things are patently going quite well. But the week by week publication of details of companies' accounts in the *Bookseller* in late 1980 and early 1981 cannot but show that many well-known and very well-established publishing houses have been having a very thin time indeed.

The problems of publishing arise from a number of causes but two major problems are mentioned in virtually every company report. Firstly the publishers have been badly hit by the strength of sterling which has made British books expensive abroad and has also reduced the value of both exports and sales of rights. The book trade can do nothing about this as the exchange rate is beyond their control. The second problem stems from considerable cutbacks in public spending on institutional books. This has arisen devastatingly in education and the Educational Publishers' Council has protested loudly and strongly about the way in which, once again, educational economies in the schools always seem to include disproportionate economies on book purchases. But higher education, which expanded between 1959 and 1979 from 164,000 to 519,600 students in full-time higher education, has also been cutting back on purchases. Universities and polytechnics, as well as other colleges of higher and further education, have all reduced their institutional purchases for libraries. Purchases of books by students cannot be adequately monitored but *ad hoc* surveys have always shown students to under-spend very greatly on the proportion of their grants allocated for book buying.

Public libraries too have been forced to make harsh economies in their book funds and a cutback here can be very serious indeed for publishers of relatively short-run hardback fiction or general non-fiction, the viability of which really depends upon a very substantial proportion of the print-run selling to libraries. Take away the library sales and many hardback-only literary novels, for example, become virtually unpublishable.

Overall, then, in the first half of 1981, at the time of writing, the book publishing industry is experiencing one of its worst recessions for many years, numerous redundancies have had to be made amongst staff, a few smaller publishing houses have closed down, some others are up for sale and not finding eager buyers, and there is more of a hope that things will 'bottom out' than any really firmly calculated expectation.

What makes life even more difficult for book publishers is the fact that their work is so much involved in producing for the future. In very general terms it can be said that a book probably takes about a year to get from the author to the reader, and so a publisher is committing himself (or herself) to putting his wares on the market at a time when he really cannot, in these very uncertain days, know what the general economy and the book market will be like. Book publishing, in general, works better in stable times, and especially in times when there is not high inflation. Scholarly publishing, for example, is really based upon the idea of printing a small number of hardback copies of a specialist monograph which will sell quietly over a period of, say, five or six years or more. Some very scholarly books have not sold out for years and years. Given a stable economy with little change in prices from year to year the rate of sale is not anything to worry about too much. But given a book published at, say, £10, with a rate of inflation of, say, 20 per cent, the price would need to be adjusted to £12 in its second year and eventually to £20.74 in its fifth year after publication if its contribution to the publishers' income needed for financing new books were to keep up with the inflationary trend.

As has been said previously in this chapter, publishing is a numbers game. It is based upon an editorial flair for picking the right book to publish in the first place, but that decision must be dovetailed into other quantitative decisions about print-runs, pricing, export sales, sales of rights and so on which are essentially business decisions. It is just as important in successful publishing to be able to get rid of books as it is to creating them in the first place.

The book publishers at the present time are faced with problems of trying to forecast for their own successes in a world economy which is highly unpredictable.

Chapter 4

BOOKSELLING

The selling of books

As was demonstrated in the previous chapter, book publishing is by no means a simple operation or industry to describe. In some ways bookselling is even more fragmented since books are sold in a variety of ways through many kinds of wholesale and retail outlets.

Without going into too much detail and thus ending up writing a textbook on bookselling, it is important to note that in the United Kingdom there are two sorts of new books sold and these are called 'net books' and 'non-net books'. The distinction is an important one because books in Britain are normally sold to the public at the net prices determined by the publishers and only under very special conditions may retailers sell to the public at less than the net price.

Retail book prices are therefore 'fixed' prices and this form of price fixing is sanctioned by law. The Net Book Agreement was defended by the book trade[1] before the Restrictive Practices Court in 1962 and Mr Justice Buckley gave the verdict for the trade on the grounds that the Net Book Agreement preserved retail price stability rather than being an instrument for fixing prices and without it there would be fewer books published and fewer bookshops in which to sell them.

The only books, therefore, which are normally sold 'non-net' are educational books sold in bulk to schools, for which suppliers are allowed to negotiate special prices. But all other books sold through conventional retail outlets must be sold at the net price. In the case of certain books sold through book clubs special discounts are allowed for what are regarded as special book club editions. During book sales, especially the National Book Sale, special titles are agreed between publishers and booksellers for reduced prices. Books can be 'remaindered' at lower prices when the end of a run is virtually being 'sold up'. But these are relatively minor exceptions to the overall general rule which results in a book costing the same price in the shops anywhere from John O'Groats to Land's End. In strong contrast to, say, television sets or instant coffee, where the consumer may save by shopping around, there is no advantage to be gained by going to one shop rather than another for a book so far as price is concerned. The customer might well get better and quicker service at one bookshop, but that is another matter.

As a result of the Net Book Agreement bookshops and other retail outlets which sell books along with other goods do not compete with each other by price wars or other means of undercutting competitors in this country, which in turn means that book buyers frequently buy books from non-bookshop outlets. Indeed, a person who, for example, buys only light romantic fiction or popular thrillers in paperback format could be a regular and heavy book buyer but never actually enter a genuine bookshop.

A definition of what a 'bookshop' really is could therefore raise problems if one wanted to be academic about the matter, though normal people usually have little difficulty in recognising that a 'real' bookshop is one that devotes almost the whole of its attention to selling books, with other goods (such as stationery) only being subsidiary lines. However, very good stocks of general books are often to be found in departmental stores and especially in the branches of W. H. Smith up and down the country and these specialist departments certainly must qualify as bookshops.

The Price Commission report on books said that[2]

over half the books published for the UK market pass directly to the retailer from the publisher without going through any system of wholesaling. Fourteen per cent of books are supplied directly to educational contractors or library suppliers; a further 22 per cent pass through wholesalers. Many of the remaining 12 per cent are supplied to book clubs and mail order houses.

By sales costs about two-thirds of books sold on the home market (which includes some imports) are for public retail sale, about 11 per cent are to schools, another 11 per cent to libraries and the remaining 11 per cent to other public and corporate bodies. Some sales to schools are made through bookshops which complicates matters further.

However, it can be seen from the above figures that whilst there is quite a substantial amount of what can be called 'institutional' bookselling in the United Kingdom, the bulk of the book trade is concerned with retail sales to individual customers. But the retail book business is considerably fragmented amongst various types of outlets and it is difficult to present a coherent picture from published data because of inconsistent classification. At the one end of the spectrum of bookselling are a number of booksellers who are members of the Charter Group of the Booksellers' Association. These people, who subscribe to rules which require them to ensure the proper training of their staff, to maintain as large as possible stocks of books in their shops, and generally to do all they can to promote better standards of bookselling, are a minority amongst the complete membership of the association, comprising (in March 1981) only 524 amongst a total membership of 3,235 of the whole association. The Booksellers' Association itself is an inclusive, rather than exclusive, trade group which works hard to improve the quality of bookselling in this country, but its members are extremely varied and include numbers of shops which would hardly be recognised as solely 'serious' bookshops. An advantage of membership is the right to trade in book tokens, which is restricted to BA members. But outlets known in the trade as 'CTNs' (confectioners, tobacconists, and newsagents) can often sell quite a variety of books, including adult and children's hardbacks as well as the popular paperbacks but not consider themselves seriously as booksellers since they do not take orders for books not in stock and leave the stocking of their book racks to the representatives of the wholesalers who supply them.

The distribution of bookshops

As it is so very difficult to give a firm definition of a bookshop it is also very difficult to give a clear picture of the geographical distribution of bookshops up and down the country. In the most general terms it is reasonable to say that most large cities have several 'real' bookshops and if a city has a university it is virtually certain to have an academic bookshop either on or off the campus. Beyond this rather obvious and expected generalisation it is difficult to go.

The capital city of London has some major general bookshops and a number of specialist bookshops which are virtually national suppliers. Grant & Cutler, who specialise in foreign languages, are a good example of the latter. At the other end of the scale most villages and small towns have some shop or shops which sell a very restricted range of paperbacks and general hardback books. In between these two extremes the variety is considerable.

When I tried in 1970 to work out a distribution of bookshops in Britain[3] I plotted the location of all the members of the Booksellers' Association of Great Britain county by county, omitting any members who were educational suppliers and so on, so as to restrict the analysis to retailers only. That piece of, admittedly, very crude research produced a map which showed the best provision of bookshops per head of the population to be in the south-east of England and the poorest provision to be in the north of England. But a county analysis is a crude instrument and, because of the small population of some Scottish and mid-Welsh counties which had a few small 'bookshops' in them, these areas actually produced some of the best ratios of bookshops to populations in the whole country. In fact, Orkney and Shetland by this analysis would seem to have had the best provision of all of bookshops per head of population!

A more discriminating analysis than the very simple county one looked at special types of towns and it was clear that seaside resorts, spas, retirement towns and administrative centres were more likely to have good bookshop:population ratios than industrial towns or railway centres. Thus Eastbourne, Worthing and Bournemouth are well provided whilst Huddersfield, Bolton, Gateshead and Rochdale are not.

This all adds up to a picture of bookshop provision being, not surprisingly, better in those parts of the country where there are more likely to be middle-class people, especially those with the leisure for reading or with occupations which may involve or stimulate reading. In the industrial north bookshop provision is less good.

To look at the question of bookshop provision in the north I carried out a study,[4] financed by the Yorkshire Arts Association, in 1974–5 which analysed in great detail the provision of bookshops in the county of Yorkshire. In this study the bookshops (defined by membership of the Booksellers' Association) were plotted against the old local government areas of county boroughs, municipal boroughs, urban districts and rural districts. Census data, mainly from the 1971 census but in a few cases from the 1961 census because of lack of data for 1971, was obtained for every area and bookshop provision was set against a number of social characteristics for areas. In addition to this the 'bookshops' were sent questionnaires asking about the amount of their business derived from the sale of books, quite a number were visited to see what they looked like and nine most helpful publishers' representatives gave me their comments on shops they visited in Yorkshire.

Taking the three ridings together (that is the North, West and East Ridings of the *real* Yorkshire before they were destroyed by an insensitive local government reorganisation) which contained a total population of just over five million people, 57 per cent lived in local government areas with 'genuine' bookshops, 10 per cent lived in areas which had only 'minor' bookshops and 33 per cent lived in areas which had no bookshops. The proportion living in areas with no bookshops was 36 per cent for the West Riding, but only 23 per cent each for the more rural North and East Ridings.

Of course, this very broad analysis contains a number of problems which must be carefully considered. A rural district could spread over a very large area of land, contain relatively few people but have a small market town in which the stationer's shop sold some books and was a member of the Booksellers' Association. By contrast an urban district could be virtually a suburb of an adjacent town, have no bookshop itself, but be within a couple of miles of a good shop in the county borough.

Nevertheless, two municipal boroughs, Batley (population 42,006) and Castleford (population 38,234), were examples of genuine towns with no bookshops. The rural districts of Flaxton (32,879), Holderness (24,311) and Beverley (31,943) also had no bookshops within their boundaries, though the small *town* of Beverley had a bookshop.

Putting together all the local government areas which did not have a bookshop in them the result was seventy-one local government areas with a total population of 1,360,812 in the West Riding, ten areas with a population of 125,141 in the East Riding and nineteen areas with 169,591 people in the North Riding.

Most of these local government areas were either urban or rural districts, some with very low populations down to just over a thousand people, and it would not be expected that they could support bookshops. What was clear from the analysis was that major population centres such as Leeds, Bradford, Sheffield, Hull and York (all of which are university towns) had what might be called 'good' bookshop provision. In smaller towns and cities, such as Doncaster, Wakefield, Ripon, Bridlington and Scarborough, people living there could expect to have one, or perhaps even two, medium-sized general bookshops, though not specialist shops. Beyond these two categories most people in Yorkshire were likely to be restricted locally to shops stocking what one representative called 'popular paperbacks and a few juveniles' if they had any book provision at all.

Clearly, then, many people in Yorkshire, as must also be the case in many parts of the rest of the country, live in local government areas – small towns or villages – with no real bookshops and must expect to travel to larger population centres if they wish to use a 'real' bookshop. To try to present a more realistic picture of Yorkshire, local government areas were combined together in what I called 'composite centres' which were groups of local government areas which clearly were satellites to local, larger towns. In this I was greatly helped by an Ordnance Survey map called 'Local accessibility: the hinterland of towns and other centres as determined by an analysis of bus services', though some local inquiries were also used to iron out a few problem cases.

As a result of this work all but seven local areas were allocated to twenty-one composite centres and it was possible to say what proportion of population for a composite centre lived in local government areas with no bookshop. This ranged from 74 per cent in the Barnsley Composite Centre to none in the Beverley Composite Centre. Amongst the centres with the largest proportions of people in local government areas without bookshops were Barnsley, Rotherham and Doncaster, which form a triangle in the south and east of the West Riding. Adding up those people in that triangle living in local government areas without bookshops produced a grand total of 528,651.

Moving a little further north, people living in local areas without bookshops in the Wakefield and the Huddersfield Composite Centres produced a total of 291,768. If these are added to the south Yorkshire triangle the result is 820,419 people in bookshop-less local government areas, which is approximately half of the complete total of 1,655,544 such people in all three ridings.

The overall picture gained from this area analysis was that the hinterlands of the industrial towns were not areas where one could hope to find much in the way of bookshops. People living in or near the largest cities would probably have quite good bookshop facilities, but for people living in what might be called industrial-rural areas the best that could be expected locally would be a moderate provision in the local middle-sized town. In more genuinely rural areas, with a smaller population more widely scattered, the position was different in some ways in that people could have longer distances to travel to a real bookshop, but even then they could only expect minor bookshop provision in the market towns. The big difference really, in the south Yorkshire coalfield, was the very large population clustered together there with no major bookshops genuinely local to them.

The geographical analysis of Yorkshire showed a lack of bookshop provision in many industrial and agricultural non-city districts. Trying to find out if bookshop provision seemed to be linked with any known social characteristics was not very productive. Using census data for age, a hypothesis that bookshops are more likely to be found in areas with more younger people had no support from the data. Analysing terminal educational age, with the hypothesis of higher levels of education being linked to more bookshops, resulted in a mixed bag of results which neither supported nor rejected the hypothesis. Looking at the Registrar General's socio-economic grades in the composite centres gave definite support to the hypothesis that the higher the socio-economic grades of the employed population the better would be the bookshop provision. This last hypothesis was the most likely to be supported and it is interesting that, in this case, socio-economic grading was a better social discriminator than was terminal educational age.

It was also worth noting that the Barnsley Composite Centre, with the poorest bookshop provision of all the centres, also had the smallest proportions in the higher socio-economic grades. This composite centre, with a total population of 291,000 people, had 74 per cent (215,606) living in local government areas with no bookshop.

Barnsley itself, a county borough of 75,395 population at the 1971 census, had at the time of this survey a medium-sized branch of W. H. Smith which had been refitted in 1974 and was well spoken of by one of the publishers' representatives. The shop gave a third of its 4,500 square feet to the sale of books and seven of the staff of twenty-seven (including part-timers) were involved in the sale of books. The only other 'outlet' at the time in the town was the branch of Boots which sold a restricted range of books. Barnsley was chosen by the Book Marketing Council of the Publishers' Association in 1980 for a large-scale experiment in book promotion. Information was collected on every aspect of life in the town that could be related to the use of books[5] and a special promotion of 'the book' was devised for the summer of

1981. As a result of the survey and a visitation to Barnsley by the members of the BMC in 1980 it was concluded that there was a strong unfulfilled desire for books in the town. Quite independently of the work of the BMC an independent bookshop was opened before the 1981 promotion so time will show if this enterprise was justified.

Bookselling as a business activity

Whilst for many book readers, and even for people involved in the book trade, books have an aura about them which makes them seem special, nevertheless the selling of books is a serious economic activity. The Price Commission report stated that 'stock-holding bookshops are the main market-place for the trade, enabling customers to examine books before deciding to buy them. They number about 3,000 out of a total of perhaps 36,000 selling outlets.'[6]

Euromonitor's Book Readership Survey for 1980[7] gave details of the volume sales of books in 1980 and 'bookshops' accounted for 22 per cent of sales, W. H. Smith for 21 per cent, John Menzies for 4 per cent and newsagents, bookstalls and department stores together accounted for 28 per cent. Most of the remainder were sold through book clubs (17 per cent) or by direct mail (5 per cent). A further analysis estimated that about half of all shops classified in official retail surveys as either 'department stores' or 'confectioners, tobacconists, newsagents' sold books. With such a vast assortment of retail outlets for books it is no wonder that there is difficulty in presenting a clear financial picture of book sales.

Estimates made by Euromonitor for the year 1979 of 'UK book sales by type of distributor at retail selling prices' give a sum of £256 million (48 per cent of the whole market) to bookshops. Leaving aside the institutional market of sales to schools and libraries which accounted for £133 million (25 per cent), wholesalers had sales of £122 million (23 per cent), book clubs £70 million (13 per cent) and library suppliers and educational contractors £85 million (16 per cent) together. However, not all *bookshop* sales by any means were restricted to individual buyers and the Euromonitor report estimates that £48 million of the £256 million bookshop sales were to libraries and educational institutions. It is clear from these figures (or perhaps unclear!) that books are sold by a wide variety of suppliers to a wide variety of purchasers and, on a national scale, it would seem as if the country is almost awash with outlets for the sale of books. But with approximately 300,000 'book' titles in print at any given time there are considerable differences between customers' demands and suppliers' abilities to provide required books on demand or speedily by special order.

One of the greatest difficulties for a genuine bookseller, and a problem which is agonised over at virtually every conference of booksellers, is the problem of fulfilling the 'single copy order' for a book not in stock, in reasonable time to suit the customer, and in a way which can provide the bookseller with a reasonable profit. It is here that the crucial difference between putting out a few popular paperbacks on a newsagent's shelves and supplying requested copies of expensive hardback books is so important and it is really the holding of considerable stocks of titles in the shop coupled with the willingness to order books not in stock that marks off the genuine bookseller from what might simply be called the book 'outlet'.

One of Britain's leading booksellers, Thomas Joy, said that 'a successful bookseller must be a good book buyer and a good businessman generally.'[8] Joy makes a strong point that whilst 'terms of supply' of books from the publishers are vital to the success a bookseller can hope for, the bookseller must actually choose the right books to sell in the first place and then be able to give good service in finding out about books for inquiring customers and obtaining books quickly which are wanted but not in stock. Obviously the better the bookseller knows his customers the more can be supplied from stock and the less needs to be ordered. Thus the good bookseller does not have too many books standing too long on the shelves and he minimises the numbers of books which fail to sell at all. 'Turnover of stock' is, then, an important part of successful and lively bookselling. In their survey of booksellers the Price Commission said that the booksellers in their sample 'turned over their stocks on average about four times a year'[9] though they added that rates of stock turnover varied widely and whilst paperbacks and library and school books could turn over rapidly, classics might turn over only once or twice a year. Yet the genuine stockholding bookseller, especially the member of the Booksellers' Association Charter Group, is committed to holding good stocks of books for the customers' benefit and this means that a good bookshop, in Charter Group terms, does not aim simply at buying in the books with the quickest turnover and ignoring the slower sellers. Such a business principle must mean that real bookselling is a combination of business enterprise and social service, and a level balance which satisfies bookseller, customer and bank manager is not easy to achieve as recent economic experience in the book trade has shown.

The economics of bookselling

The Charter Group of the Booksellers' Association, the 'elite' group of about 500 firms in Britain who could be considered as the core of genuine booksellers in the country, have carried out an annual economic survey of themselves since 1964. In recent years they have been helped in this work by staff of the Manchester Business School. The survey depends on returns (which are treated confidentially) from members and the data supplied are carefully analysed both to give trends from year to year and also to make comparisons between firms of different sizes. The annual surveys contain a wealth of information which each bookseller can use to help him both compare himself with his peers and also to see where the problems of bookselling are looming at the present time.

The results which claim the most attention are those which analyse sales and profitability for the contributing bookshops according to five sizes of shop. For the 1979/80 survey,[10] which was derived from 346 questionnaires representing 410 shops, the sizes of the five equal-sized groups were as follows:

Category	Book sales
Small	£56,000 and below
Small/medium	£56,001–£101,000
Medium	£101,001–£152,000
Medium/large	£152,001–£305,000
Large	over £305,001

For the trading year being surveyed the net profits from book sales and the proportions of shops with profits or losses from book sales are shown in Table 4.1. As the commentary on the 1978–9 survey said, 'there is a very significant association between size and profitability: the bigger the business, the greater the likelihood of achieving a better than average net trading profit.' The 1979–80 survey noted that 'there are again signs of polarisation'. The net profit is no more than 3.8 per cent at best with the large bookshops but is down to a loss of 0.7 per cent for the small ones, amongst whom well over 40 per cent have run at a loss over the past year. However, there are some problems of what the figures show as the 1978–9 survey report commented in two sections that 'the way in which the survey treats notional salaries' for both the small and the small/medium bookshops could be producing some distortion.

Table 4.1

PROFIT AND LOSS 1979–80

Size of book sales	% net profit overall	% of shops with net profit on year	% of shops with net loss on year
Small	(0.7)	55.5	44.5
Small/medium	2.5	73.4	26.6
Medium	3.9	75.3	24.7
Medium/large	4.6	88.6	11.4
Large	3.8	87.2	12.8

The percentage of shops making a loss declined slightly to 24.1 per cent from 25.1 per cent in the previous year, though the 1979–80 report notes that 'although more shops have made a net trading profit, the level of profitability has fallen.' Interestingly, the proportion of loss makers amongst the large category of shops declined from 13.8 per cent the previous year to 12.8 per cent for 1979–80, but for the medium/large shops the decline was from 21.6 per cent to 11.4 per cent. For 217 businesses for which comparable data were available, the gross profit was the same at 29.1 per cent for 1978/9 and 1979/80 but the net (trading) profit was down from 3.6 per cent to 3.1 per cent.

The general picture given by the Charter Group surveys, year by year, is none the less one of a considerable struggle to survive on the part of many booksellers, especially the smaller ones. With a continuing recession in 1981 the picture to be expected from the next survey when it is published could easily be worse as the *Bookseller*, during 1981, reported severe trading problems amongst a number of well known bookselling firms.

Before leaving the problems of making a living from bookselling it is interesting to take note of one last set of figures in the surveys which give some details of the actual composition of total sales made by the Charter Group shops. These throw an interesting light on the different ways in which bookshops of various size make their livings. Table 4.2 gives details.

As this table shows, the larger bookshops do a considerably higher proportion of their business with libraries, whilst the smaller bookshops do rather more business with book agents (who could well be local school bookshops and the like). Sales to schools are fairly well spread, though the medium-sized shops seem to do slightly more business with them. It is very interesting though to see that the small and small/medium shops make about a fifth of their sales from goods other than books, and for the small shops this figure rises to nearly a quarter of sales. In a very detailed table, in which each category of bookshop is divided into 'low', 'average' or 'high' profitability within the category, the shops selling higher proportions of other goods are better represented in the 'high' profit sections for the three categories of

Table 4.2
COMPOSITION OF TOTAL BOOK SALES AND OTHER GOODS

% of book sales coming from	Small	Small/ medium	Medium	Medium/ large	Large
Retail	85.6	84.9	81.7	72.5	75.8
Library	4.1	5.4	7.4	14.6	17.0
Book agents	2.3	1.6	1.4	0.6	0.4
Schools	8.0	8.1	9.5	12.3	6.8
Total book sales	(100)	(100)	(100)	(100)	(100)
Books as %	77.3	80.1	83.1	85.0	86.9
Other goods as %	22.7	19.9	16.9	15.0	13.1
Total all Sales	(100)	(100)	(100)	(100)	(100)

small, small/medium and medium-sized shops. Table 4.3 shows these figures.

The most striking figure in Table 4.3 is the 43.9 per cent of sales coming from goods other than books in those small bookshops which were in the one third of all the small shops categorised as 'average' for net profit. It has to be said that there were only fifty-seven shops altogether in the 'small' bookshop category and

Table 4.3
PERCENTAGE OF 'OTHER GOODS' SALES BY OVERALL PROFITABILITY

Size of shop	Low	Average	High
Small	31.1	43.9	31.1
Small/medium	19.9	24.8	20.3
Medium	14.4	15.9	24.6
Medium/large	15.3	11.4	24.9
Large	19.7	12.5	16.9

the 'average' were only twenty-two shops altogether, but even so over 40 per cent in the 'other goods' category must surely indicate that for these shops the sale of goods other than books was possibly a life-saver. It is also noticeable that all three sizes of shops, medium, medium/large and large in the 'high' profits class, sold more 'other goods' than those with 'average' profits. Bearing in mind that 44.5 per cent of all the small-sized shops had run at a loss *on book sales* in the year surveyed it must follow that trying to make a living by selling books in a small bookshop in the present time is a very difficult business indeed. One cannot but be reminded of a description of the relationship between a father and his daughter in a melodrama of 1841 entitled *The Beggar's Petition, or A Father's Love and a Mother's Care*. The father, Old Brightwell, curses his daughter, Jane, for preferring the love of the smooth-tongued villain, Grandley, to that of her own parents. But the curse has no effect and, as the commentator says, 'Ten years later his daughter Jane is still Grandley's mistress and the Brightwells are reduced to keeping a little bookshop in London.'[11] It is to be hoped that they sold a few 'other goods' as well.

Bookselling as an occupation

As has already been shown, there is a considerable range of business activities concerned with the selling of books and many traders who are, in varying degrees, involved in the 'selling of books' would certainly not lay claim to being thought of as 'booksellers'. Some of the things that are said about genuine bookselling do at times seem to elevate this occupation to a level far beyond mere commerce. As Schücking wrote of the trade, 'The bookseller is concerned with a more noble form of merchandise than any other and he is thus an aristocrat among traders. If he is to fulfil the high tasks of his calling he must be at one and the same time a scholar and a businessman.'[12]

Thomas Joy, a devoted bookman himself, wrote that, 'Bookselling is more than a trade – it is a vocation. Few booksellers regard their shops simply as money-making enterprises: they believe good bookshops are at least as much a cultural necessity as the public libraries.'[13] Certainly, in spite of relatively low wages and a career structure which has few very well paid managerial posts even at the very top, bookselling does seem to attract to it people who would seem to be prepared to work as shop assistants in bookshops who would not consider working as assistants in, say, grocers' or dress shops.

In his statement Thomas Joy does, of course, refer to booksellers and 'their' shops, which implies the viewpoint of either a proprietor or a manager rather than a sales assistant. Nevertheless simply working in a bookshop is, as any customer can readily see, the sort of full-time or part-time occupation which can be taken on by middle-class people without loss of social status. In a survey I carried out in 1970–1[14] in which 257 people working in bookselling were interviewed up and down the country 74 per cent had fathers whose occupations were non-manual and either middle or lower-middle class; 44 per cent were in categories A or B, as used by market researchers, which indicates professions and higher or middle management. As the national distribution of these classes at the time was only 12 per cent for the A and B group or 29 per cent for the ABC_1 group, it is clear that the people in bookselling came very disproportionately from a middle-class background.

Only 26 per cent of the people working in bookshops had left school at the age of 15 or less, and for proprietors of shops the figure was only 14 per cent. Interestingly also, 61 per cent of all the people had been educated at independent or grammar schools and 30 per cent had gone on to some form of further or higher education. Just over half of the sample of people were under the age of 30, with the more junior assistants on the whole being fairly young people. Overall, 44 per cent of the 257 people interviewed had begun their working lives in bookselling. When these people were asked why they had gone into bookselling the variety of reasons given was interesting. Table 4.4 gives details.

As this table shows, it is impossible to say that there is any clear path which leads to bookselling since for some people it is simply

Table 4.4
REASONS FOR ENTERING BOOKSELLING
AS FIRST JOB (IN %)

Reason for entry	
Generally interested in books and literature	15
Had actually looked for jobs in bookselling	13
Suggested to them by teacher or careers officer	11
Alternative to entering librarianship	14
Family connections already in bookselling	15
Simply answered an advertisement for a job	22
Wanted retailing work	6
Others	4
	100

a job, for some it is the hoped-for start to a career and for some it is obviously part of a family business. I commented in the report that 'bookselling appears to attract a great variety of people'.

When asked about the similarities between bookselling and other forms of retailing the answers given by respondents were very enlightening. More than a third of people said that bookselling was quite different from any other form of retailing and, whilst 23 per cent accepted that because it was *selling* it must be like other retailing, 9 per cent mentioned particular problems of stock control, 7 per cent instanced special relationships with customers and only 11 per cent felt that bookselling was really just like any other retail trade. Bookselling was felt to be more complicated than many other forms of trade, particularly with the thousands of titles that could be requested and the problem of knowing one's own stock. The need to establish relationships with customers, to be able to provide help and information and to provide for people's cultural and educational needs were all felt to be important and, with these needs, it was felt that bookshops differed in having a better type of staff in the shop.

Respondents in the survey had few unrealistic ideas about bookselling itself and many commented that they did not work in bookselling simply for the money alone, that promotion prospects were not always good and that it was a job that would not suit everybody. But many felt it was fascinating, in spite of problems, and that there were great satisfactions to be derived from being able to cope well with customers (a point stressed by a majority of respondents) as well as having a good knowledge of books themselves. About two-thirds of the people in the sample felt they could probably earn more money in another sort of job, but equally about two-thirds expected to stay in bookselling.

At about the same time as the study of people in bookselling was being made I also carried out a small investigation[15] in four secondary schools in Sheffield to find out how young people, aged about 15 who were in classes where most pupils would be expected to leave at 16 with some 'O' levels, felt about the prospects of working in a bookshop. The pupils (110 in all) were asked, during an English period, to write an essay on the question, 'How do you feel about the idea of working in a bookshop when you leave school?' The essays were carefully analysed, using content analysis techniques, to see what the young people felt about an occupation which, the essays made clear, few knew anything about and few had considered for themselves at all.

In writing about what they should do in looking for jobs many young people stressed the need to *avoid* jobs for which they felt they would personally be unsuited. This rather negative aspect clearly coloured some of their views when it came to thinking about bookselling. A few writers made some reference to bookselling and librarianship having points in common. A knowledge of, and a feeling for, books were both recognised as desirable qualities and the ability to get on with people and to exercise patience were also noted. Curiously, though, in writing about what they thought bookselling actually entailed the task most mentioned was dusting and tidying, followed by helping people and then knowing the stock. Only twelve of the 110 essays made any mention of the fact that booksellers themselves have to buy in the books they sell and only eighteen writers (mainly from middle-class backgrounds) mentioned stock-taking.

Bookshops themselves were described in ways which showed that young people knew that *actual* bookshops were quite often airy, well-lit and very pleasant shops to visit, yet the stereotypes of 'stuffy', 'dusty', 'fusty' and so on were still clearly strong in their minds. Mention also was made of an expectation of quietness, if not absolute silence, in the shop and customers were stereotyped as old people, intellectuals, uninteresting people, shy or stuck-up people and people afraid of life. The other staff with whom the young people would work in the shop were seen as middle-aged, stuffy, dull and uninteresting. The son of a salesman actually wrote, 'I should imagine that one's fellow workers could be classed as dull, uninteresting cast-offs who have a flair for English.'

The most positive advantage of working in a bookshop, mentioned by fifty-seven essay writers, was that it enabled people to *read* books and a further twenty-nine thought that it would broaden the mind. But forty-four mentioned poor prospects, twenty-eight mentioned low pay, twenty thought the work would be very tiring and a surprising twenty-nine said they would not like to work surrounded (in some cases even 'hemmed in') by books all day. Even more curiously thirty-three essays mentioned a *lack* of customers.

Experiments of this kind, asking young people to write about things of which they really have very little knowledge or personal experience, are most valuable in revealing the stereotypes which people have in their minds. It was clear from the analysis of the essays that many young people knew very little at all about how bookshops operate and that working in a bookshop was something they had never considered for themselves. But the survey did reveal, very startlingly in places, that these young people had some strong prejudices against bookshops which bore little relationship to reality. One young girl gave a vivid picture which almost sums up the problem. She was the daughter of a labourer, but she herself reads and actually buys books. She wrote,

The atmosphere of a bookshop I always imagine to be stuffy and fusty. I should imagine that each time a book was removed from its shelf a cloud of dust would choke the air. The shop itself would be tiny and dark, hidden away in an alley-way. Of course I know that many if not the majority of bookshops are clean, large and modern but I think the picture framed in my mind has turned me against even considering working in a bookshop.

With such strong prejudices against bookshops as were expressed by the young people in this study the question must obviously be asked – what is a *real* bookshop like and who are the customers and how do they behave in the shops?

Bookshops and their customers

With so many different types of bookshops and shops of all sizes up and down the country it is absolutely impossible to say what a 'typical' bookshop customer is like. The people who regularly browse the shelves of Blackwell's in Oxford can hardly be expected to be closely similar to those who shop at the W. H. Smith's branch in Barnsley.

First of all it is salutary to consider whether people use bookshops at all. I think it would be a rare adult who has never been into a bookshop in his life and I would guess that most people have bought a book of some sort during their lives. So to try to estimate how many people 'never' buy books or 'never' go into bookshops is a difficult empirical task. It is probably more accurate and down-to-earth to use statistics which deal with relatively short periods of time for which people can be expected to have a clear memory.

From their own surveys Euromonitor[16] estimated that the average purchase of books per month per household in the UK in 1979 was 0.77 of a book. They also estimated that 54.5 per cent of households bought no paperbacks and 63.2 per cent of households bought no hardback books. But they have to admit that, as their annual surveys are in effect spot checks done only once a year, and the 1979 survey was made in January when people have Christmas money and book tokens to spend, there must be seasonal variations which could affect the overall picture quite strongly. Nevertheless, the Euromonitor 1980 report cites 53 per cent of men and 58 per cent of women saying that they were not reading a book of any sort at the time of the survey, and most reading surveys give a figure of about 40 per cent of all adults as non-book-readers.

One cannot expect people who do not read books at all to be avid bookshop customers, even though they may perhaps buy the odd book as a present for someone else, therefore it would seem reasonable to infer that, at best, probably only about half the population uses bookshops at all. In the 1980 survey, when asked if they had bought any books in the last *month* 68 per cent of all men and of all women said they had not, with the proportions being larger for older people and working-class people. This figure compares closely with a figure of 62 per cent of all adults who in a 1974 survey[17] said they had not bought a new book from a shop over the past twelve months. If we accept, then, that bookshop customers are a minority of the general population we can next go to consider what they do when they are in bookshops.

For many years there was a severe lack of objective and systematic information about behaviour of people in bookshops and though I had myself published[18] the results of studies I had made in an academic and a general bookshop, both of these were case studies from which it was difficult to generalise. In these two surveys, the one of Dillon's University Bookshop in London and the other of A. B. Ward's (now Bowes & Bowes) general bookshop in Sheffield, the users were seen to be predominantly male, young rather than old, containing a good proportion of students (expected at Dillon's but 36 per cent even at Ward's) and, on the whole, mainly middle-class with a good educational background if they were beyond the student stage. In both shops about half the customers were hoping to buy a book or books, a few were dealing with orders and over a third were simply browsing around the shelves. At Dillon's 43 per cent and at Ward's 62 per cent of people went out neither having bought or ordered a book. An analysis was made of the books purchased by customers at Ward's and the variety of books was very wide indeed, with non-fiction and rather more 'practical' books predominating.

A more recent, large-scale, national survey[19] commissioned jointly by the Book Marketing Council of the Publishers' Association and the Booksellers' Association has, at last, given a detailed picture of people's purchasing habits in general bookshops. Although the report's title is 'Lost Book Sales' the study is much more positive than that and gives a great deal of valuable information on actual buying behaviour, with lessons to be drawn about loss of sales from these data. The survey, in which 3,131 people were interviewed at fifty-one general bookshops in England, Scotland and Wales, involved an interview with the person on entering the shop and a second interview as he (or she) left. This excellent technique enabled the survey workers to say definitely, rather than speculatively, whether a customer had actually got what he wanted from the visit.

The report divided people entering the bookshops into three categories. The Definites, who made up 24 per cent of those interviewed, went into the shops with a definite book in mind to purchase. The Possibles, who were 23 per cent, were looking for a book on a subject or a book by an author without an exact specification. The remaining 53 per cent were Browsers who went into the shop without any definite intention of buying a book at all (and actually 44 per cent of them were planning to buy items other than books). In round figures, half the Definites went out without buying or ordering the book they wanted; about a third of them did buy their planned book. Over half the Possibles went out without buying a book. About a fifth of the Browsers did buy a book.

In all 20 per cent of visitors went out with a book they had intended to buy, 15 per cent went out with a book they had not intended to buy and 67 per cent went out without buying at all. (A few went out with both intended and unintended purchases.) It was interesting to note that 13 per cent of the Definites did not buy the book they had intended to buy, even though they found it in the shop, and usually this non-purchase was because of the price. Also one-third of the Definites were looking for books as gifts for other people, mainly for relatives.

Turning to the books themselves, there was almost an equal three-way split in their purchase: 36 per cent of the books were bought by the Definites, 34 per cent by the Possibles and 30 per cent by the Browsers. In total 47 per cent of all books bought were impulse buys and this comprised 42 per cent of books sold by cash value. Another most interesting finding was that 82 per cent of all the books sold were paperbacks.

In fact, of all the books sold 34 per cent were fiction and 17 per cent were children's books. Of fourteen other categories of books used for analysis the highest was domestic science with 6 per cent. Not surprisingly, the Browsers were greater buyers of fiction than the two other categories. As the report itself says, 'Those with Definite ideas for books, and those using Charter bookshops, are rather more likely to buy non-fiction, to buy in hardback and to spend more money per book. But even among the most "serious" groups . . . the main (book) group remains fiction in paperback.' It was also worth noting that 'among those buying books as presents, 59% bought paperbacks, 41% hardbacks.'

The customers themselves had demographic profiles which will come as no great surprise to most book researchers. Of these, 57 per cent were women, 74 per cent were under the age of 45 (with 30 per cent under the age of 25) and 70 per cent were social class ABC$_1$. Differences between the Definites, the Possibles and the Browsers were not very great at all, though there were more men Browsers.

The 'lost book sales' were very carefully analysed with the help of the shop managers and these affected 11 per cent of the customer sample – people who left the shop not having bought a book they intended to buy. The survey categorises 45 per cent of these lost sales as 'unsatisfiable demand', half of which stems from inability to identify the books the customers believed they wanted and the rest from the books not being published, not in paperback, out of print or seen and rejected. The other 55 per cent of lost sales were mainly because the books wanted were not in stock though some were on order but had not been delivered and an interesting 6 per cent of all lost sales were books on the shelves or in the stock-room but not found by the customer. The report estimates that, if the unsatisfiable demand is excluded, then lost book sales are the equivalent of 16.6 per cent of all total units sold and the equivalent of 25.9 per cent of current retail sales value. It is said in the conclusion that for every £1,000 spent in the bookshops (of which £590 is on planned purchases and £410 is on impulse buys) customers were looking for books worth:

£26   which were in the shops but not found by them,

£41   which were on order,

£192 which were not on order (by the bookseller).

This survey, which in my opinion is probably the most thought-provoking study yet commissioned by the book trade, contains a wealth of information, some of which is very detailed, but some of which, excellently presented by the writers of the survey, gives a remarkably clear and simple picture of customer behaviour. For example, in the summary of findings it is explained that in every 1,000 people (entering a bookshop):

670 are likely to leave with no books at all.

130 are likely to come in with a definite book in mind and to leave with 165 books (including books specifically ordered for them).

110 are likely to come in with a possible book in mind and to leave with 162 books.

90 are likely to come in to browse or to buy something else but to leave with 129 books.

From Browser, to Possible, to Definite the average costs of books bought rose from £1.54 to £1.70 to £2.21, with over three-quarters of sales in paperback form. Looking at the money spent again the clear statement explains that of every £1,000 spent in bookshops:

£282 is spent by Definites on books they planned to buy,

£77 is spent by Definites on books specifically ordered for them,

£88 is spent by Definites on books not originally planned to buy,

£231 *is spent by Possibles on books they planned to buy,*

£75 *is spent by Possibles on books not originally planned to buy,*

£247 *is spent by Browsers on books not originally planned to buy.*

Thus, £590 in every £1,000 is spent on planned purchases, £410 on impulse purchases.

Bearing in mind that this was a survey of *general* bookshops, and thus specialist and educational bookshops were excluded, it is not surprising to find fiction and children's books looming so large in the purchases, though perhaps the emphasis on fiction and on paperbacks does just tend to obscure the fact that *one* very expensive hardback book on, say, art could give the bookseller many times more profit than would *one* popular paperback thriller. Nevertheless, the survey is invaluable in indicating so clearly the types of customers and the way they behave.

This survey shows that roughly one in three of all people who enter bookshops go out with a book or books, which can be regarded as disheartening or amazing according to one's own view of the function of a general bookshop. It is perhaps most disheartening that half the Definites went out of the shop having neither bought nor ordered, though clearly they could be going on to another bookshop. In fact 13 per cent of Definites did find what they wanted but did not actually buy, with too high price as the main reason cited for rejection.

Amongst the Possibles 55 per cent did not find what they wanted and 7 per cent found something suitable but rejected it – again mainly on grounds of expense. It was interesting to note that amongst the roughly a fifth of Browsers who bought a book the most frequently mentioned reason for having bought (24 per cent) was to give the book to another member of the family.

The importance of books as gifts is something that has been noted in several surveys. Apart from the obvious popularity of book tokens of which over 1.5 million to the value of nearly £6 million were sold in the year ending January 1981 it is estimated from surveys that one in five of all books bought are purchased for other people and the figure is one in four for women buyers.[20] However, an older survey carried out for a book trade working party in December 1973–March 1974 (which obviously covered the Christmas period) found 54 per cent of purchases to be for other people and a very high 75 per cent of all hardback books to be for others – 63 per cent being for children.[21] The more recent lost book sales survey asked the 24 per cent of people who went into bookshops with a 'definite' book in mind to purchase why they wanted to buy it and 31 per cent of these people said they were wanting to buy the book as a gift. But the 20 per cent of the 'browsers' who originally entered the bookshop without any intention of buying a book (and browsers were more than half of all those people interviewed) but did go out buying a book also bought quite a number of books as gifts. No less than 24 per cent of the browsers who bought, who can therefore be said to have been impulse buyers, bought the book or books to give to another member of the family.

The lost sales survey is not absolutely specific about books bought as gifts amongst its three categories of customers. Whilst the survey does state that one in three of all people entering the bookshop with a definite book in mind were seeking gifts, the picture is not as clear for the 'probables' and 'browsers', though it does say that 'it may well be that gift buyers represent at least a similar percentage of indefinite and impulse buyers'. If this were so then, clearly, a third of all bookshop customers would be gift seekers, which might well be a reasonable estimate. It must be noted that the Euromonitor survey giving 20 per cent of *books bought* is not restricted to purchases from genuine bookshops, as is the lost book sales survey. The book trade research survey also dealt with general purchases, not restricted to bookshops only. The statistics vary according to the way they have been collected, where they have been collected and when the surveys were made, but all indications point to the same general conclusion, that an appreciable amount of all books sold are bought as gifts for other people.

The books people buy

With perhaps as many as 300,000 titles in print, and with the *Bookseller* using forty-six different categories for classifying types of books published, it is clear that anyone buying a book could be buying from a bewildering variety of offerings. Many purchases of books by students, academics, businessmen and so on are purchases of specialised books for their work and I shall not deal here with those aspects of book buying. In the general book market, however, there is still a great deal of variety in purchasing habits. The lost book sales survey, analysing 1,679 books bought, classified 34 per cent as fiction, 17 per cent as children's books, 6 per cent as domestic science, 4 per cent as biography and the remaining 26 per cent under twelve various headings such as natural science, history, art and so on, none of which accounted for more than 3 per cent each. Of all the books bought 82 per cent were paperbacks, which is a very high proportion indeed of the total books. The figure was as high as 86 per cent in paperback amongst the browsers who bought.

The 1980 Euromonitor survey said that 64 per cent of the books bought by 'adults who had bought a book in the last month' were paperbacks (and for women purchasers the figure was 69 per cent). This survey said that 21 per cent of purchasers had bought at a 'specialist bookshop', 24 per cent at a branch of W. H. Smith or Menzies and 16 per cent through a book club. The remaining 39 per cent had bought their books at newsagents, bookstalls, department or variety stores and other such 'outlets'.

Not surprisingly these people's buying covered an enormous range of both fiction and non-fiction, with 52 per cent of purchases fiction and 48 per cent non-fiction. Crime/thrillers accounted for 10 per cent of all purchases and romance for 9 per cent (though 15 per cent amongst women). Educational books made up 10 per cent overall (though 15 per cent amongst men), and modern novels (6 per cent), historical fiction and history (each 5 per cent) were also popular. It must be noted though that only 76 per cent of respondents said they had bought the books for themselves, so this survey finds virtually a quarter of all book purchases bought as gifts.

There is a bit of book trade folklore that says that people buy non-fiction and borrow fiction from the libraries, but, like most folklore, this is not really true. People buy vast quantities of paperback books, and amongst those paperbacks there are large numbers of fiction books – as the sales of romantic fiction, historical fiction and crime/thrillers well show. It can be argued that the popularity of the paperback book and the ease with which it can be sold attracts non-bookshops to selling them and makes life just that bit more difficult for the genuine bookshop which also stocks the less-easy-to-sell hardback books. Nevertheless, it has never yet been seriously argued that there should be restrictions placed on any retail outlets wishing to sell books, so long as they honour the Net Book Agreement, and, as we shall see in the next chapter, the ordinary reader who simply wants to *read* a book without having to *buy* it has one of the finest library services in the world to supply his or her needs.

Chapter 5

THE LENDING AND BORROWING OF BOOKS

The background to lending

In a famous paper given at the eighteenth congress of the International Publishers' Association in 1968, R. E. M. Van den Brink,[1] a Dutch publisher and book researcher, gave an international review of 'Book Reading, Borrowing and Buying Habits' which brought home to publishers everywhere, but especially British ones, the importance of borrowing as a source of books. Van den Brink produced many statistics for European, American and Asian countries to show the differences between them but probably the most striking of all were the histograms showing the differences between books bought and books borrowed per household per year. France was the easy leader for countries where more books were bought than borrowed, but when it came to countries where more books were borrowed than bought the United Kingdom had no serious rival.

Van den Brink worked out a borrowing/buying balance for books related to the number of books per literate person in the 10 to 65 age group and, whilst for France the ratio was a reverse one of 3.79 in favour of buying, for the United Kingdom the borrowing/buying balance was 15.56 in favour of borrowing, with Turkey second at 8.37 and the Netherlands a low third at 2.55. He then concluded, in his analysis of the data, that in the United Kingdom 'borrowing is so strong with respect to buying that the economic growth of publishing could quite possibly be hindered'. Van den Brink's conclusion is open to serious debate, since the economic viability of many short-run books depends upon library purchase and, of course, as has already been shown, British publishing depends a great deal for its livelihood upon successful exports and sales of rights. Nevertheless, Van den Brink's paper lent weight to the feelings often expressed by people in the book trade, especially booksellers, that Britain's excellent 'free' library service has produced a nation of people who expect to borrow their books rather than buy them. Actually, Van den Brink's figures showed the UK to be very low compared to other European countries such as Holland, Germany, France and Belgium in the percentage of its gross national product spent on books, so the total expenditure for Britain on books from any purchasing source is, according to his data, nothing for Britain to boast about. But the important element in the comparative data is the great imbalance in Britain between buying and borrowing amongst the general population and this must be related to the provision of libraries in Van den Brink's figures, since there is no suggestion anywhere in his paper that borrowing and lending privately between individuals has been considered at all. In fact such private transactions had, in 1968, hardly been considered in international statistics.

Libraries in Britain

In spite of the picture of a nation of book borrowers suggested by Van den Brink's data, the Euromonitor survey for 1980[2] gave book purchases by the public in 1979 as £400 million compared to £54 million spent by public libraries and £11 million spent by universities. Local authorities spent £68 million on books but, of course, much of this would go to the purchase of school textbooks rather than library stock. The publication *Public Library Statistics, 1979–80 Actuals* from the Statistical Information Service of the Chartered Institute of Public Finance and Accountancy (CIPFA)[3] gives the total expenditure on books by public libraries in England, Wales, Scotland and Northern Ireland as £46,860,764, which amounted to 17 per cent of the total costs of the public library service in the UK for that year. In a total turnover of nearly £600 million, £47 million is not a vast amount of money, but it must be remembered that the annual expenditure on books made by public libraries is for new books to add to an already very impressive stock of books available to the general public.

Britain may claim to have led the world with its first Public Libraries Bill of 1850, though this, as McColvin[4] pointed out, 'was a very modest measure, authorising town councils to expend not more than the product of a rate of one halfpenny in the pound on libraries, but *not* on books which were to be provided voluntarily by the local population.' The latter part of the nineteenth century certainly saw a great interest in library development, in which Carnegie was prominent, but neither the limitation of expenditure on libraries to a penny rate nor the lack of legal authority for county councils to provide libraries were removed until 1919. With the local government reorganisation of 1974 many local libraries became parts of the 166 current library authorities of the UK which, in 1979–80, had a total expenditure of nearly £274 million, and an income of nearly £11 million. The 'free' library service is quite a costly business, though many would argue that it gives an excellent service for what it costs the nearly 56 million people for whom it works.

In fact, in 1979–80, a total staff of 29,352 people, of whom only 8,150 were in professional posts, ran a total of 4,888 libraries, 702 mobile libraries and 10,838 outlets categorised as 'homes, hospitals etc.' with a total library book stock of 135,049,000 volumes.[5] This stock works out at, per head of population, 2.41 volumes in England and Wales, 2.60 in Scotland and 2.96 in Northern Ireland. During the year the nearly £47 million spent on books worked out as an expenditure per head of population of 82 pence per person in England and Wales, 91 pence in Scotland and £2.53 in Northern Ireland. When one considers that United Kingdom expenditure in 1979[6] on social security was £18,500 million, on health and welfare £11,100 million and on education £9,500 million, the whole of the public library service expenditure can be seen to be a very small part of the nation's social provision. The total stock of books held by 162 library authorities supplying data to CIPFA for 1979–80 was, as has been said, just over 135 million volumes. Unfortunately only 137 library authorities were able to supply detailed information on the types of books available for loan which they hold in stock, but Table 5.1 shows the breakdown for these 137 and the 96 million volumes they hold. A total of 146 library authorities reported holding 14,842,000 reference books which were not available for loan. As Table 5.1 indicates, there is more non-fiction available for loan than there is fiction, roughly speaking six non-fiction to every five fiction.

Table 5.1

LENDING STOCK BY TYPE
(137 LIBRARY AUTHORITIES)

Type	Number (millions)	%
Adult fiction	34.844	36.2
Adult non-fiction	41.754	43.4
Children's	19.679	20.4
Total	96.277	100

Interestingly, the additions made to lending stock during the year reported to CIPFA by 140 library authorities showed a balance in favour of fiction, as Table 5.2 indicates. In addition to the above, 142 library authorities reported the addition of 587,292 reference books and 163 library authorities (only three short of the complete total) were able to report a total addition of 13,998,110 volumes in all, which works out as 0.245 new books per head of population in the year for England and Wales, 0.257 in Scotland and 0.459 in Northern Ireland.

The preponderance of adult fiction over non-fiction purchases is not something that has just happened in the last year or so. As Table 5.3 shows, the proportions of purchases between the three categories has altered steadily over five years even though there have been fluctuations in the total numbers of books bought.

Table 5.2

ADDITIONS TO LENDING STOCK 1979–80
(140 LIBRARY·AUTHORITIES)

Type	Numbers	%
Adult fiction	4,518,881	43.2
Non-fiction	3,083,756	29.5
Children's	2,861,067	27.3
Total	10,463,704	100

Table 5.3 shows a slight but steady increase, year by year, in the proportion of adult fiction bought from 1975–6 to 1979–80. It is a pity that the first two years of the table covering 1975 to 1977 contain lower numbers of authorities supplying data to CIPFA, but even so the percentages indicate for the whole five years that the proportions of books bought for children have been extraordinarily steady for four of the five years, only dipping at all appreciably in the last year of 1979–80. Between adult fiction and adult non-fiction however the change, though not huge, is nevertheless a progressive one. The slight trend towards the buying of more fiction over these five years has not yet been sufficient to tilt the balance of the overall lending stock

Table 5.3

ADDITIONS TO LENDING STOCK 1975–6
TO 1979–80

Year	Adult fiction	%	Adult non-fiction	%	Children's	%
1975–6 (123)	3,675,516	39.7	2,962,320	32.0	2,616,475	28.3
1976–7 (131)	4,117,592	40.8	3,118,094	30.9	2,850,335	28.3
1977–8 (140)	4,141,337	41.2	3,090,536	30.8	2,816,774	28.0
1978–9 (141)	4,735,081	42.1	3,357,139	29.9	3,148,055	28.0
1979–80 (140)	4,518,881	43.2	3,083,756	29.5	2,861,067	27.3

held by the libraries, as the 1979–80 figures still showed (as Table 5.1 has indicated) adult non-fiction to comprise 43.4 per cent of all lending stock compared to 36.2 per cent for adult fiction, but if the trend continues in its same way the total lending stock held could be predominantly fiction by about 1985. Such a redistribution of lending stock would reflect more the pattern of borrowing as indicated by all empirical data.

The borrowing of books from libraries

The CIPFA annual surveys give two sets of data for lending. The first is an overall figure for the annual issues of books for the whole year and the second is the cross-sectional picture of books on loan at a particular time – in fact on 31 March.

The first set of data, for annual issues for 1979–80, was as shown in Table 5.4. The total issues per head of population for the year were 11.9 per person in England and Wales, 11.2 in Scotland and 8.0 in Northern Ireland, which is an interesting reversal of the rank order of countries for both stock held and expenditure per head of population.

Table 5.4 is interesting in the way that it shows the overwhelming popularity of fiction for borrowers, with not far from three fiction books borrowed to every one of non-fiction. When one notes that only 36.2 per cent of the total lending stock is fiction,

Table 5.4

ANNUAL ISSUES IN 1979–80 (134 LIBRARY AUTHORITIES)

Type	Number in 000s	%
Adult fiction	317,393	59.9
Adult non-fiction	116,291	22.0
Children's	96,041	18.1
Total	529,725	100

but 59.9 per cent of the total lending done is of fiction, the importance of the demand for fiction is highlighted.

The second set of figures, for loans as at 31 March 1980, reduces the percentage of fiction from 59.9 per cent to 52.4 per cent in the cross-sectional analysis but this table is of more value in showing how, at a given time, certain proportions of stock are out on loan. Table 5.5 shows this. Table 5.5 is extremely interesting in that it shows, firstly, that at any given time (if 31 March is not untypical) just over half of all books on loan will be adult fiction and, restricting the picture to adult books only, nearly two out of every three books on loan will be fiction. When one considers what proportion of the total national stock will be on loan on a given day, adult fiction is far ahead of the other two categories, with over 40 per cent of stock out on loan. In fact, since the on-loan figures are derived from data from 128 library authorities and the total lending stock figures are derived from returns by 137 library authorities, the figures in Table 5.5 are, if anything, likely to be a little on the low side.

Table 5.5
STOCK ON LOAN AS AT 31 MARCH 1980
(128 LIBRARY AUTHORITIES)

Type	Number (in 000s)	%	% of that total stock on loan
Adult fiction	15,267	52.4	43.8
Adult non-fiction	7,925	27.2	19.0
Children's	5,945	20.4	30.2
Total	29,137	100	30.3

Of course, it could be argued that some non-fiction books are used for reference rather than people necessarily wanting to borrow them, but in answer to that it must be stressed that the whole of the above analysis is based upon the CIPFA figures supplied to them related to lending stock only; the nearly 15 million reference books reported to be held by 146 library authorities do not come into this analysis at all, which is wholly restricted to lending and borrowing from the libraries. Unfortunately the CIPFA figures do not (and it must be presumed could not) give any data on the use of reference books within a library which could only be monitored in open access libraries with great difficulty and at very high cost.

Whilst the analysis of annual issues for 1979–80 gave over eleven issues per head of population for the year for England, Wales and Scotland, the analysis of stock on loan as at 31 March gave the books on loan on that day as 0.68 per head of population in England and Wales, 0.62 in Scotland and 0.53 in Northern Ireland. So, for every man, woman and child in the country, which must, of course, include babes in arms, illiterates, the blind and so on, at any given time there is no more than an average of about two-thirds of a book on loan from the so-called 'free' public library service. Such a tiny figure is simply the result of rather crude percentaging. Some people never use public libraries at all whilst some are regular, heavy borrowers. Statistics such as are collected by CIPFA do not, and cannot, take account of the variables needed for estimating the social usage of libraries. In the next section we turn to look at what is known of the use made of public libraries by people wanting to borrow books.

Book borrowers

The only regular social survey which can give a national picture of book reading and borrowing habits in the United Kingdom is the Euromonitor annual readership survey. In the 1980 edition 55 per cent of a national sample of 2,000 men and women over the age of 16 said that at the time the survey was being done and they were being interviewed they were not 'reading a book currently'. The 45 per cent who were reading a book (or books) were asked how they obtained their current book and two sources stood out above all the rest. In the lead were 38 per cent of people who had borrowed their book from a library and 30 per cent who had bought the book (including buying it from a book club). Borrowing from friends or relatives accounted for a further by no means inconsiderable 16 per cent, whilst 10 per cent of books currently being read were gifts to the reader. These figures thus indicate that at any given time about two out of every five books being read by the 'adult' population come from libraries – and it is fair to assume in a survey which uses a sample drawn from the general population that virtually all of this library borrowing will be from the public libraries.

The Euromonitor table[7] shows women (40 per cent) as being greater library borrowers than men (34 per cent) and borrowing reaches a peak at 47 per cent with men and women aged 55 or over. Not surprisingly the AB social class group also lead in borrowing at 43 per cent, though it should not be overlooked that the figures for the C_2 and the DE groups (the two working-class categories) were 39 per cent and 38 per cent respectively, which shows them to be only slightly below the AB group. If the figures for library borrowing in this table are reworked so as to provide a 'profile' of the social class of the library borrowers the result is that, of all those people who said their current book had been obtained from a library, 44 per cent would be social class ABC_1 (middle class) and 56 per cent would be C_2DE (working class), thus giving a predominance of working-class borrowers over middle-class ones. Admittedly, this profile is derived from only 335 people in a complete sample of 2,000, but it *is* derived from a carefully taken national sample and there is no alternative national library borrowing survey which can produce contrary evidence.

In the field of research into book reading the use of public libraries has been studied more than other activities such as book buying and general reading habits, largely because interested, and often very hardworking, librarians have carried out surveys for themselves of their local catchment areas in the hope of providing better library services for their communities. The study by Martin L. Ward[8] published in 1977 brought together 126 different studies carried out over the years 1900 to 1976 in Britain and Ward tried his best to draw together the extremely varied findings and give a general picture of reading habits and library use. It is no fault of Ward's that some findings were difficult to reconcile since methods, categories and terminology used showed the sturdy independence of the true Briton and, of course, findings for, say, a county area with a widely dispersed library system and readership would hardly be expected to produce identical results with, say, an *ad hoc* survey of one branch or central library in an inner London borough. Ward's study is likely to remain a standard reference source for years to come, but trying to sort out the generalities from the particularities is a very difficult business. In the following paragraphs I have used Ward as the background against which to highlight certain aspects of borrowing by the use of selected examples.

If one had to make a gross generalisation about library borrowers it would be along the lines that they are more likely to be women than men, middle-class rather than working-class, reasonably well educated and a bit older rather than younger. The problem is that there is always a survey which can produce different findings and the 'general' library user, as a 'national' character, does not really exist. People use local libraries which cater for local interests. One major survey[9] carried out between 1971 and 1972 in selected areas in south Cheshire, north Staffordshire and Lincoln, which collected data from nearly 50,000 library users, produced conclusions such as, 'In proportion to their representation in the population as a whole, the most use of libraries was made by those aged 65 and over and by children between the ages of 5 and 14.' This finding would seem to fit reasonably well with the Euromonitor 1980 figures[10] which gave 43 per cent of the people who said that their current reading had been obtained from a library as being aged 55 or more.

However, the important point about library use has already been touched upon a few paragraphs above. There can only too easily be confusion in the use of statistics which deal with two different concepts — those of 'profile' and 'penetration'. For example, in the Midlands survey it is true that the 65 and over age group were, as an age group, the heaviest users of local libraries, with a figure of 85 users in every 1,000 population in the 65+ age group. The figure for the 5 to 14 age group was 79 per thousand and both of these *proportionate* figures were better than, for example, the 45 to 64 age group with 64 per 1,000 or the 15 to 19 age group with 66 per 1,000. These figures indicate a greater degree of penetration in library use amongst the young and the old. But when one looks at the *profile* for age of all those people who are library users the 65 and over group fall in importance and, comparing the same size of age groups where one can, the younger to middle-aged people in the 25 to 44 age group become more important. Table 5.6 shows the two factors together.[11] (It must be noted that the penetration figures per 1,000 appropriate population merely reflect the proportions of the 48,000 people surveyed. They should not be read as meaning, for example, that only 85 people exactly per 1,000 of the *whole* population of 65 and over for this area are library users. Yet another trap for the unwary!)

In Table 5.6 both the profile and the penetration figures are of importance and both, in their different ways, are 'right' in what

Table 5.6

PROFILES AND PENETRATION OF LIBRARY USERS (IN %)

Age Group	Profile of library users	% of Population in survey areas	Penetration per 1,000 population in age group
Under 5	1.4	8.2	11
5 to 9	6.8	14.6	79
10 to 14	10.4		
15 to 19	8.2	8.3	66
20 to 24	6.9	6.9	67
25 to 44	26.9	25.7	70
45 to 64	24.1	25.3	64
65 and over	14.1	11.1	85
No answer	1.2	—	—
	100		

they say. It all depends on what the reader of the statistics is wanting to get from them. If one discounts the under-fives (who might well have been excluded from the calculations) it can be seen that the user profile is not a bad reflection of the total population profile for the area and so the local librarians could with justice congratulate themselves on providing a library service which does cater in fact, and not just in theory, for all ages. When we look at the penetration figures (which, of course, do not add up to 100 per cent since this is not a frequency distribution but is a set of proportions) we see the differences between user profile and population profile picked out for us. For example, the 65 plus age group is 11.1 per cent of the population but 14.1 per cent of the users and so penetration is relatively high at 85 per 1,000. The 5 to 14 age group of users is 17.2 per cent compared to 14.6 per cent of the total population, so the penetration is here at 79 per 1,000. From these figures, the local librarians can see that their services are doing rather better with the older and younger readers than they are with the age groups in between. These are simply comparative ratios which tell one story. The *total* penetration of the library services in the whole population is not given in this table since the data come only from a sample of users. To find out about complete penetration requires a different survey, sampling the whole population.

Surveys of the total penetration of libraries in the general population usually produce two sets of data. The one is of people who are 'members' of libraries and the other is of people who are 'users'. Normally users are subsumed under members, though in the use of reference material users may not be members in some cases. In the report on the Hillingdon project,[12] which covered Uxbridge, Hayes and Ickenham libraries, Totterdell and Bird said that 49 per cent of the total population from the age of 14 had current library tickets, though this varied from 35 per cent in Hayes, through 48 per cent in Uxbridge, up to 73 per cent in Ickenham. It was estimated however that 54 per cent of the population had used the libraries in the past year, though 18 per cent had not used them for reading material. It was further estimated that another 29 per cent had used the libraries, though not in the past year, leaving only 17 per cent of the whole population who were believed never to have used the library system at any time.

Usage in Hillingdon would seem to be at a fairly high level compared with some other areas. A report on library services in Greenwich[13] in 1974 said that between 40 and 43 per cent of the local population aged 15 and over in this borough used the library, but for eleven other London boroughs cited the average figure was 34 per cent. Ward[14] looked at twenty different surveys which gave membership rates and came up with an average of 27.5 per cent, with extremes as low as 4.6 per cent in one Hull district and as high as 58.4 per cent in an area in Derbyshire. National figures for either membership or usage are, to a large extent, speculation since no national membership figure is published and even if one were published it would include many people who have tickets but rarely if ever use them. User figures must come from sample surveys of the general population and here there is always the margin of sampling error and, one suspects, a tendency for people interviewed to overstate their use of public libraries. Probably a figure somewhere between 30 and 40 per cent of the adult population are library users, with the figure for real users nearer the 30 and to include less regular users nearer the 40.

The social background of users

When considering such social indicators as social class and educational attainment with regard to book borrowing it is very important indeed to keep clear the distinction between profile and penetration. Virtually every survey which analyses data by class or education emphasises that people in the higher classes, or with higher levels of education, tend to be greater readers, are more likely to be book buyers and use libraries more.

For example, in the Greenwich report it was said that[15]

The 60% of the population who do not use the service is disproportionately made up of the less well-educated, less well-off, more disadvantaged sections of the community. For example, people who left school before seventeen are four times less likely to use the library as those who stayed till eighteen and eight times less likely as those who took further education.

However, it must be remembered that, roughly speaking, there are two working-class people to every one middle-class person in our society and about three-quarters of the population cease their education at the minimum school-leaving age. So, allowing for the weighting towards the lower categories in the profiles of both class and education, it can be seen that there is sense in McLellan's statement that, 'All investigations indicate that the use of libraries is much higher *proportionately* (my italics) among the better educated, but that *quantitatively* the number of the poorer educated using libraries is as great if not greater.'[16]

These differences are very clearly brought out in the results of the Hillingdon survey where the provision of the raw data has enabled me to give profiles to add to the authors' data on penetration.[17] As Hillingdon would seem to comprise quite a large amount of middle-class residential areas the class profile of

Table 5.7

LIBRARY USERS IN PAST YEAR BY SOCIAL CLASS, HILLINGDON

Social Class		Penetration % using in past year	Profile % Distribution of users
1	Professional etc.	73	11
2	Intermediate	69	31
3a	Non-manual skilled	65	19
3b	Manual skilled	46	32
4	Partly-skilled	29	6
5	Unskilled	13	1
			100

Table 5.8

LIBRARY USERS IN PAST YEAR BY TERMINAL
EDUCATION AGE, HILLINGDON

TEA	Penetration % using in past year	Profile % Distribution of users
21 and over	89	15
18–20	78	12
16–17	76	33
15 or under	39	40
		100

users is very high, with 61 per cent in the first three groups (which is just about double the national population figure) and a high 15 per cent of people have received education to the age of 21 or beyond. However, this does not matter too much since the tables are being used here to illustrate the fact that the rate of penetration must be related to the proportion of the group concerned in the overall distribution. Thus the highest social group (here designated as class 1, professional etc.) has a high penetration figure of 73 per cent, but itself comprises only 11 per cent of all the users. The class 2, intermediate group has 69 per cent penetration but at 31 per cent of all users is just below the 32 per cent of class 3b, manual skilled which has a penetration of only 46 per cent. Unfortunately the Hillingdon data are not completed by the provision of class and educational profiles for the whole population of the area, including non-users, but the penetration and profile comparisons indicate clearly enough that Hillingdon libraries' clientele is about 40 per cent working-class and about 40 per cent educated only to the minimal level. This is a very substantial minority of the users even though penetration of classes 4 and 5, the partly-skilled and unskilled manual groups, is still low.

A national sample survey carried out in 1974 for Book Club Associates[18] gave comparisons of the age, social class and educational levels for public library borrowers and the general public in Great Britain. These data are interesting in showing how the age profile for regular library users is slightly skewed towards older people and distinctly skewed towards the middle classes. Table 5.9 gives the details. As this table shows, the age profile for all borrowers is very close to that of all adults in the country but when one looks at the more frequent users, the regular borrowers, the older people come more to the fore. In general though the age profiles for all borrowers and general population show that, for this variable, the public libraries really are 'public'.

Table 5.9
AGE, SOCIAL CLASS AND EDUCATION OF LIBRARY USERS IN %

| | *Public Library* | | |
	All borrowers	*Regular borrowers*	*Adults in Great Britain*
Age			
15–19	8	5	9
20–34	25	22	26
35–44	21	20	20
45–64	24	26	25
65+	22	27	20
Social Class			
AB	20	20	14
C₁	30	30	22
C₂	26	24	31
DE	24	26	33
Education			
Degree	10	9	6
'A' level	10	7	6
'O' level	17	18	13
None	55	57	69
Not stated	8	9	6

Note: Regular borrowers use a library at least fortnightly.

The social class distribution, not surprisingly, shows the greater use made of the library service by the middle-class (ABC$_2$) people, but, even so, whilst the C$_2$DE people make up 64 per cent of the total population they are still 50 per cent of the library-user population. So, by these data, the public library service can be said to be serving all the social classes.

The profiles for education are interesting in showing that, whilst better-educated people, not surprisingly, tend to use libraries proportionately more than lesser-educated people, there is a slight fall away of graduates and 'A' level holders amongst the regular users. Perhaps this might be explained by the fact that some more upper-class and highly educated people, whilst being library users, also have many other activities and thus find themselves a little short of time for regular reading. Any explanation though of this aspect of the data is, at present, purely speculative.

The general data which give information about the characteristics of library users are incomplete without also having data on what people use libraries *for*. Public libraries offer a variety of services and, from a user point of view, a great deal of library usage is concerned with the *selection* of items for use and borrowing. We now turn to look at this.

Borrowing as an activity

In their very large sample survey in the Midlands Taylor and Johnson asked public library users for their reasons for using the library they were at,[19] and Table 5.10 gives these reasons, which total more than 100 per cent as some respondents gave more than one answer. 'General recreation or leisure' stands out head and shoulders above all the others, though it should be noted that the first three items (marked with asterisks) which are of rather more serious intent tended to be given more frequently at central libraries and the 'general recreation and leisure' was down to 53.7 per cent at central libraries, though up to 67.3 per cent at 'other' libraries. The picture, then, is fairly clear in showing

Table 5.10

REASONS FOR USING LIBRARY:
MIDLANDS LIBRARIES SURVEY IN %

Occupation or work	7.3*
Formal course of study	9.0*
Personal activity or hobby	20.9*
General recreation or leisure	63.7
On behalf of someone else	11.3
Other reasons	2.7
Total	114.9

central libraries providing for a fairly even balance between the more serious and the purely recreational interests, whilst the other (presumably branch) libraries were two-thirds devoted to general recreation and leisure.

Taylor and Johnson's figure of 11.3 per cent of users being there 'on behalf of someone else' raises a point which is all too seldom discussed as a feature of the public library service. In his comparative study of borrowing, Marsterson[20] pointed out that 29 per cent of people in his own survey of Maltby, 28.5 per cent of people in Luckham's surveys of Chester and Eccles and even 13 per cent in Mann's survey of the Sheffield central lending library were seeking books for other people. At Maltby 10 per cent of the respondents were borrowing for people who never went to the library at all. The importance of proxy borrowing is surely something which should be considered more in relation to the information and advice made available for borrowers by librarians themselves.

However, reverting to the main features of Table 5.10 it must also be noted that Taylor and Johnson amplified the importance of general recreation and leisure as a reason for library use by saying that 'two thirds of all adult library users who were borrowing books for themselves said they would be looking for any novel of interest'. In fact the figure was 65.4 per cent overall, down to 52.3 per cent in central libraries, but up to 72.4 per cent of borrowers at 'other' libraries. The importance of this finding surely cannot be ignored, pointing as it does to the fact that two out of every three borrowers in all public libraries and virtually three out of every four in branch libraries are looking for fiction – and looking for 'any novel of interest' in that search.

The Euromonitor survey for 1978,[21] which gave 53 per cent of all men and 39 per cent of all women not borrowing books from the local library, also noted that 70 per cent of all men and 72 per cent of all women said they never used the reference facilities in their libraries, and only about 5 per cent of all respondents said they used the reference facilities 'regularly' as opposed to 'sometimes' or 'never'.

All these findings emphasise the importance of the lending facilities of the libraries and, within lending, fiction is the foremost category. It is impossible to evaluate the comparative importance of reference and borrowing activity since so little is known as yet about the total behaviour of people in libraries. Whilst one reference made by a scholar to the local history collection may be of considerable value in his or her research another one made in the general reference section may simply be to an issue of *Which?* for the latest comparisons of instant coffee or ironing boards. A borrowing of a non-fiction book could be the autobiography of a near-illiterate footballer ghosted by a hack journalist, whilst a fiction volume borrowed could be a novel by one of the outstanding writers in the English language. Statistical categories are perforce crude tools for the evaluation of quality. At the present time all we can do is to pick our way through what statistics are available from surveys and hope that the inferences that we draw are not too removed from the actuality behind the numbers.

In his survey of the Maltby library in Yorkshire, serving a local community of about 15,000 people, Marsterson inspected 674 books that were being borrowed and classified 7 per cent of them as being for study, 10 per cent of them as being for practical purposes (hobbies, sport, etc.) and the remaining 83 per cent as being leisure reading (including non-fiction, such as biography, travel, war stories, etc.). In my own survey of the Sheffield

Central Lending Library[22] the use made of it by students and rather more 'serious' borrowers produced a figure of 25 per cent of 1,045 books borrowed being for work, 11 per cent for practical interests and 64 per cent for leisure reading. The rough figure of two-thirds of borrowing or borrowers for leisure or relaxation seems to come up time and again in surveys.

Unfortunately there are few surveys of any size which give complete details for all borrowing of fiction and non-fiction, though the general picture is of most fiction borrowed being what is known as 'light' fiction and in the wide array of non-fiction available such categories as 'biography', 'travel', 'education', and 'history' usually get the most mention, though men borrowers often add books on business and technical subjects.[23] In Luckham's surveys in Chester and Eccles[24] he found 72 per cent of people borrowed fiction, but within that group only 8 per cent borrowed what he classed as 'serious/classical' fiction. In a study of Cumbria adult fiction lending [25] which analysed 18,000 issues it was found that 58.8 per cent of adult fiction issued was what the librarians called 'light' fiction, made up of romance, detective stories, westerns and historicals of a non-serious type.

Perhaps one of the most interesting and illuminating of local library surveys was the one carried out by Luton public libraries where of 843 books borrowed by 382 readers 603 (72 per cent) were fiction. Over a third of the fiction was mystery stories of one sort or another, a fifth was romances and nearly one in ten was a historical novel. The analysis then went on to say that[26]

216 people (57%) said they borrowed only fiction and 79 (21%) said they borrowed only non-fiction. Moreover, 116 of the fiction readers (54% of fiction-only readers) borrowed only one type of fiction. Even more surprising, 57 of the 79 non-fiction-only readers (72% of this group) borrowed only one type of non-fiction. It is evident that the vision of the public library user as a person of catholic taste is a little askew.

Unfortunately I have not been able to find another survey which incorporates data which would support or contest the conclusions of the Luton survey, but there is no evidence that refutes the predominance of 'light' fiction in the general fiction borrowing that is done.

The borrowing of fiction

There can be no serious argument against the predominance of fiction in the borrowing from public libraries. The CIPFA national book statistics indicate the enormous amount of fiction borrowed, national readership surveys confirm this and every individual library survey supports it. The bread and butter business of public libraries, especially branch libraries, is the lending of fiction. Yet, although God and Dewey between them seem to have decided that books divide into two main categories of fiction and non-fiction, no satisfactory classification of fiction has ever yet been arrived at which could be compared with the elaborate yet universally accepted method devised for non-fiction by Dewey.

The conventional 'classification' of books in public lending libraries is a basic division between non-fiction and fiction, with non-fiction shelved according to the Dewey decimal system (which few borrowers will ever have heard of) with perhaps a major category such as autobiography and biography hived off as a completely separate *ad hoc* classification. Fiction is conventionally shelved in alphabetical order of the authors' surnames, with short stories perhaps dealt with as a further sub-section at the end, after Z. There are some libraries that have special shelves set aside for fiction categories such as 'romance', 'detective', 'western', and a few others and some libraries use small stickers affixed to the spines which have cartoons or ideograms indicating a special genre. A heart on a pink background thus indicates 'romance' (rather than medicine) and a magnifying glass or a gun might indicate a detective story – though a gun might mean a 'western' if it is a revolver and a war story if it is a field gun. Books thus labelled may be either segregated into separate shelves or integrated within the general fiction stock.

The important thing though is that the prime base, from which genre categorisation is only an offshoot, is shelving alphabetically by author. The assumption, therefore, on the part of librarians *must* be that borrowers seek for books according to the names of the authors if the books are thus displayed for the benefit of the readers. Of course, the books are not displayed *primarily* for the readers' benefit; they are actually shelved alphabetically because this is the *only* way anyone has ever devised for keeping all the fiction neat and tidy on the shelves in a way which enables the library assistants to return books to 'their proper places' and in a way which helps those people who *do* seek for authors and titles to find them (if they are correctly shelved). Since some people do actually seek for fiction by title and author, or by author, rather than simply browsing along the shelves hoping for something to catch their eye, the alphabetical system is of help to the more purposeful borrower who might just as well be helped if he (or she) knows what he is looking for since no help at all (apart from genre labelling) has yet been invented to help genuine browsers.

If most people were purposeful borrowers the present system would be democratic in applying to the majority of users. Unfortunately no surveys have yet indicated that the majority of fiction borrowers do know what they are looking for. For example, a 1977 survey carried out in Upton library by Cheshire County Library[27] found 22 per cent of borrowers who said they were looking for a 'specific book' and 25 per cent who said they were looking for a 'specific author', though it is not clear if these are discrete or overlapping categories – one feels overlapping is the more likely. However, an enormous 89 per cent said they would be satisfied by some 'alternative choice'. When asked if they were successful in finding books they had been seeking 41 per cent of the borrowers said they had been unsuccessful. When further asked what action they had taken then, 20 per cent said they had asked the staff, 7 per cent had reserved a book, but 43 per cent had taken the 'same type of book' and 29 per cent had taken a 'different type of book'. These figures hardly suggest a desperate urgency amongst borrowers for precisely the one book that matters.

In a survey carried out in Sheffield Central Lending Library by

Nicholas Spenceley[28] he asked 100 people borrowing or return-ing 135 serious modern literary novels why they had borrowed particular books. A very small 4 per cent had reserved that particular title, 13 per cent said they had looked for that specific title, 46 per cent said they looked for books by that particular author, but 37 per cent said they had borrowed the book simply because it looked interesting on the shelf. It must be stressed that Spenceley's survey was restricted wholly to serious modern novels and that 'popular' fiction was excluded. What is therefore all the more surprising is the fact that more than a third of these books were borrowed with author and title unknown.

When the borrowers of twenty-two books which were just being borrowed (not returned), author and title unknown, were asked why they had decided to borrow these books, in eighteen cases the borrowers said that the title had caught their eye, which is a very logical answer since a book shelved spine out in a library only really declares its title, author and perhaps publisher. In fact two people of the twenty-two had borrowed a book of which they thought the author's name was vaguely familiar (and they had got the wrong author). Most borrowers, seventeen in all, had read the blurb on the jacket and twelve had dipped into the text before deciding to borrow, so there was some sampling of these unknown books before the borrowers decided to take them out. Nevertheless a figure of 37 per cent completely 'blind' borrowing of literary novels is not a matter to be ignored. It can be argued that for people to come across new authors and books they have not heard of before is an important part of the work of public libraries. People can be encouraged to sample new authors as it costs them nothing to try and this is one important function of 'free' libraries.

To see how people had enjoyed the novels they had borrowed Spenceley asked fifty people who were returning sixty-two novels about their reactions to them. Among the sixty-two books three (5 per cent) had not even been started and a further fourteen (22 per cent) had only been partly read, leaving forty-five (73 per cent) which had been read from start to finish. The three un-started books were set aside and the borrowers of the rest were asked a number of questions, using a printed prompt list to help them, about their positive and negative reactions to the books. For example, positive reactions included, 'It was an enjoyable experience', 'It made me think' and 'I found it sad but not depressing'. Negative reactions included, 'It was no more than a time filler', 'It was dull' and 'I found it depressing'. Taken together the positive responses (and readers could give more than one if they wished) accounted for 60 per cent of all responses and the negative ones for the remaining 40 per cent. What was especially interesting though was the relationship between the response to the book and the reason for having chosen it in the first place. Table 5.11 gives the details. This table surely tells a fascinating story. When the book had been reserved or if both author and title were already known satisfaction was virtually assured. If the author was known but not the title the odds in favour of a positive response were two to one. But if the book had simply been picked by chance there was a three to two chance of the reader responding negatively.

Table 5.11

REASONS FOR CHOOSING AND REACTIONS TO
59 LITERARY NOVELS (IN %)

	Positive Reaction	Negative Reaction
Title reserved	100	0
Author and title known	92	8
Author only known	67	33
'Just looked interesting'	40	60

So, the conclusion which seems reasonable for one to draw from this piece of research is that if borrowers in public libraries get hold of serious modern literary fiction without knowing in advance anything about the author or the title there is a more than even likelihood that they will be disappointed with their 'choice'. It could therefore be argued that more guidance should be offered in libraries which would enable borrowers to select more wisely and to match better their interests to the books on offer. In his conclusions from this piece of research Spenceley comments that subject specialists in libraries are now common-place in educational libraries and in the non-fiction areas of public libraries, but there are very few librarians who are fiction specialists in spite of the tremendous amount of lending of this type of book.

Whilst Spenceley's study focused particularly on the serious modern literary novel another study by a student of libra-rianship, David Spiller of Loughborough University,[29] looked at fiction in general in four different libraries in Loughborough, Leicester, Finchley and Hendon. Spiller interviewed people re-turning novels and, of 1,314 novels returned, he decided that 79 per cent were 'recreational' and 21 per cent were 'serious' according to a very careful *ad hoc* categorisation he developed for the survey. He too found that, amongst his sample of 500 readers, there was a high degree of specialisation, with 65 per cent borrowing only recreational fiction, 16 per cent borrowing only serious fiction and only 20 per cent of the sample who borrowed both sorts. (He also found 14 per cent of the borrowers had chosen books for other people.)

Spiller's largest categories of fiction borrowed were 'mysteries' (27 per cent), romances (12 per cent), historical novels (10 per cent), adventure stories (9 per cent) and what people simply called 'good stories' accounted for 10 per cent. He also went into quite a lot of detail in asking the borrowers how they had come to choose the books. When they were asked simply to choose between 'author' and 'browsing' for the books they were return-ing when being interviewed it emerged that 54 per cent of books were chosen for author and 46 per cent were chosen by browsing. When the respondents were asked how they usually went about choosing novels to borrow there was a great deal of combining which is best shown in Table 5.12. This table is surely a very important finding in indicating how extraordinarily varied are borrowers' ways of selecting their fiction. The balance between author and browsing is almost perfect, with one-third favouring

Table 5.12

HOW BORROWERS USUALLY CHOOSE NOVELS (IN %)

Author only	11
Authors/some browsing	22
Equal authors/browsing	36
Browsing/some authors	20
Browsing only	11
	100

authors, one-third favouring browsing and the remaining third favouring them both equally.

It could be, and indeed often is, argued that 'browsing' in a library is a good thing for people in that it gets them away from the narrow interest, opens people up to new authors and new viewpoints and in so many ways is what people should be doing in libraries. The problem is that browsing can be such different things for different people. For example, I know personally of a borrower who is so well versed in modern fiction that he will borrow a novel published by a Duckworth author unknown simply because he believes that Duckworth the publishers are an enterprising house who try to encourage little-known novelists of some quality by publishing their books. But is this very sophisticated means of selection really 'browsing'? As Spiller commented in his study, 'a "browsing only" approach was often dictated by ignorance of what was published, or inability to remember authors' names'.

When Spiller followed up the act of browsing by asking people about the things that influenced them in their browsing activity he found that it was difficult for people to describe what happened and a certain amount of prompting, in which cases, publishers, blurbs and titles were mentioned, was needed to help out respondents. Allowing for a certain 'pushing' that these four items might have brought about it was nevertheless very interesting to find that 27 per cent of people said 'the visual impact of the cover design influenced them to pick up the book in the first instance' and 19 per cent said they were 'attracted in the first instance by the title of the novel'. 11 per cent said that the reputation of the publishers sometimes affected their choice, though this seemed to be largely restricted to Gollancz 'yellow back' novels, Collins Crime Club and Mills & Boon romances. These fairly low percentages do not give a very clear picture of why people actually *took* a book off the shelf in the first place since there were overlap answers and even 27 + 19 + 11 only adds up to 57 per cent. However, 78 per cent of the borrowers mentioned the blurb and this was usually the most important factor in the making of the choice. As Spiller comments,

Librarians enjoy criticizing blurbs and blurb-writers, and it is perhaps easy to overlook the value of having a brief summary, on the book itself, of the main features of a novel. At the same time, the blurb is obviously not the ideal tool for this purpose. It is aimed at members of the reading public and booksellers as a selling medium, not necessarily concerned with reading satisfaction.

Although Spiller has a point that blurbs may be written to sell books it is inescapable that the blurb is virtually the only guide that a vague searcher has to guide him or her about the content of a 'strange' book.

In all the surveys of borrowing that have been published the importance of browsing and the importance of blurbs always comes up. Both of these factors only emphasise that so many people walking round the shelves in libraries really do not know what they are looking for. When students and research workers are trained to use academic libraries they are quickly told that browsing is an inefficient way of acquiring knowledge. Indexes, abstracts, catalogues, bibliographies and so on, leading all the way to computer data bases, are set forth as the modern, time-saving and efficient ways to obtain information. Now no one (I hope) wants to move recreational reading onto computer-based searches. People who are wanting to read books (and especially fiction books) are interested in *reading*, not information seeking. The act of fiction reading in particular is an act which gives intrinsic satisfaction. When one is reading *for* some purpose then the reading immediately becomes extrinsic in its function. The difference between reading *for* something and just reading is important. It could be argued that it is impossible simply to 'read', full stop. Even the lightest of light fiction is read for something – for relaxation, for distraction, for escapism, perhaps even for filling in the time between birth and death. But empirical observations from the library surveys strongly suggest that much book selection is almost without purpose. If two-thirds of the borrowers in Taylor and Johnson's surveys in the Midlands could really just be seeking 'any novel of interest' then the amount of interchangeability between titles which this phrase suggests is enormous.

It does therefore seem reasonable to conclude that book borrowing, and especially the borrowing of fiction which is so great a part of all borrowing, is an extremely haphazard business. From some points of view this could be a good thing if people, purely by accident, stumble across books written by the finest writers in the world. One would like to think of happy people who had, in their almost random browsing behaviour, been attracted by the design on the spine of a book with a fascinating title such as *A Severed Head* and had thus become great readers of Iris Murdoch. But would such readers be drawn to a novel with the title *The Sea, The Sea* which sounds as if it could be yet another of those genre-type naval adventure stories? Would anyone seriously be attracted to a book with a title such as *Quartet in Autumn*? Serendipity, surely, is something which can happen to the individual, but is a strange basis for library planning.

One can only conclude from all the evidence in surveys that libraries are still, for the main part, run by people called librarians who understand complicated non-fiction classification systems and who are only marginally interested in fiction for people who have no knowledge of non-fiction classification and, in any case, are more interested in fiction. The problem then has to be resolved as to who the libraries are really being provided for – librarians or borrowers. If, as has been claimed by some analysts, public libraries are really only bringing a quarter of the public into their libraries then the question must be asked – why do the other three-quarters of the population stay away? Certainly it is not because they have so many books of their own that they do not need libraries. The pity is that, as Totterdell and Bird showed in the Hillingdon survey, more people are actually in favour of libraries than actually use them. Too often libraries are for other people.

My conclusion is that public libraries have still a long way to go before they are fully accepted by the general population. I am not suggesting that everyone should become a bookworm – there are plenty of healthy, happy and good people who do not want to read books and their right to *not* read must be respected. But I do believe that the research data indicate that the people who do now go into libraries could be helped more in their wanderings amongst the books. Browsing when one has no clue what one wants is not a very intellectual activity, it is rather aimless meandering.

The need for good, simple information which could *help* borrowers in deciding what to look for is surely the general inference to be drawn from the research. So few libraries seem even to pin up review pages of the Sunday papers, list recent book-prize winners or give any reminders to borrowers about books that have been in the news. As for author catalogues which could help readers by cross references to other authors (Reeman, Douglas – if you like his books why not also try Callison, Brian; Kent, Alexander; Forester, C. S., or even Conrad, Joseph!), such things do not seem to exist and some libraries do not even consider fiction to be important enough to have an author catalogue at all. Van den Brink showed Britons to be the biggest borrowers of books in the world, and yet there seems so much potential for better borrowing by an even wider range of borrowers.

Chapter 6

BOOK READERS

Introduction

There are always problems associated with research into book reading which arise from the difficulty of determining what is meant by 'reading' and what constitutes a 'book'. The Euromonitor 1980 Survey[1] gave 45 per cent of all people over the age of 16 (42 per cent of men and 47 per cent of women) as reading in that they had answered 'yes' to the question, 'Are you reading a book currently?' The readers were fairly evenly distributed by age categories but were skewed towards the upper groups for social class in the proportions of each category reading 'currently'. In the 1979 Euromonitor Survey[2] reference is made to the 1977 General Household Survey which showed 54 per cent of all adults (52 per cent of men and 57 per cent of women) claiming to 'have read a book in the past four weeks'. With this wider definition one would expect the proportion of readers to be higher.

But, even if we accept from these two surveys, which are only examples of numbers of reading surveys, that roughly half the population do read books, what does this mean? A person could 'currently' be reading, or in the past four weeks have read, *War and Peace*, a Mills & Boon romantic paperback, an introduction to thermodynamics or a biography of Winston Churchill. The only thing one can really find in common between such disparate books is that they are printed words bound in book form which, for communication purposes, require a literate user. What the reader is reading the book *for* and what he (or she) actually gets out of the book requires an understanding of the purposes to which books are put by readers.

The situation of readers is akin to that of listeners to radio or viewers of television, indeed to all forms of mass communication where there is a medium of communication which can be employed for widely different purposes. It is not necessary here to go into the McLuhan argument that the medium is the message for one to understand that communication via the printed word is different from communication via, say, the television screen and that the social implications of the 'electronic journal' which might only ever be 'printed' on a visual display unit are tremendous. Considering only the conventionally printed and bound book we can appreciate well enough that reading is a skill which requires a certain standard of literacy, but *appreciation* of a book depends upon many personal qualities. Thus a Mills & Boon romance is likely to be read by a young or middle-aged housewife who is simply seeking distraction from her daily chores,[3] but the same romantic novel could be read by a scholarly literary researcher interested in this type of work as a popular literary genre.[4]

The application of what is usually called the 'uses and gratifications'[5] perspective to the media of communications applies a variety of possible questions to any communication according to the uses to which it is put and the gratifications which ensue for the user. I have myself attempted a model for the use of books,[6] which is based on a work–leisure continuum, in which the functions for which books may be used become the essential criteria for discriminating between types of books – from 'pure' work to 'pure' leisure. But whilst one can for the most part be safe in saying that a specialist monograph on neural surgery is not *intended* to be written or published for light recreational reading and conversely a 'James Bond' type of thriller is not seriously intended as a scholarly analysis of the British secret service, too little is yet known about people's motives for reading for any researcher to be sure why, for example, most people who read serious modern literary fiction do so. We are, as yet, still not far beyond the stage, which should always come first in research, of *describing* what people do. If our descriptions are good then they can be illuminating and hypothesis-provoking and can lead on to further sound empirical work rather than just speculation or assertion.

What then *is* known of people's reading habits? Who reads and what do they read?

Reading habits

Once again the Euromonitor surveys are the only sources in Britain which attempt to give a national picture of reading habits. When, in the 1980 survey, the 45 per cent of adults (that is, for these purposes, people aged 16 and over) who were 'currently' reading were asked what they were reading the question was put in the form, 'What subject is the book you are currently reading? Is it fiction or non-fiction?', and the interviewer was instructed 'AND PROBE FULLY FOR SUBJECT'. The categorisation for entering responses on the interview schedule then gave eleven types of fiction and twelve types of non-fiction, each with an additional category of 'other' for books which the interviewer could not assign to any of the pre-set categories. The categories used were as follow:[7]

Fiction	Non-fiction
Romance	*Encyclopaedia/atlas/dictionary*
Historical	*History*
Crime/thriller	*Biography*
Classic	*Cookery*
Humour	*Sport*
Horror/occult	*Arts/craft*
Science fiction	*Religion*
Western	*Business/technical*
War/adventure	*Travel/guides*
Modern novel	*Educational*
Children's	*Gardening/DIY*
Other	*Leisure*
	Other

The survey results showed that, for the 45 per cent of people who were reading, fiction was considerably ahead of non-fiction. All together 65 per cent of responses were for fiction and 37 per cent were for non-fiction (the excess over 100 per cent is due to a few people citing more than one book). But whilst three-quarters of the women claimed to be reading fiction, only half the men were reading this type of book. Differences between the two categories for age and social class were not very great, though (perhaps contrary to popular belief) the older people were reading a little more fiction and (as one might forecast) the middle-class respondents were reading rather more non-fiction.

But within the categories used by Euromonitor there were the most interesting pointers. For example, of the 75 per cent of women's reading accounted for by fiction, 'romance' was 25 per cent and 'historical' was 16 per cent, the equivalent figures for men being only 1 per cent and 6 per cent respectively. Romance was particularly popular with the older and more working-class readers, whereas historical books were rather more popular with middle-aged readers and the more middle-class.

Amongst men the most popular fiction genre was the category 'crime/thriller' with 16 per cent readership, slightly more popular with the middle age groups but not having any strong social class bias. 'War/adventure' accounted for only 7 per cent of readers, only just ahead of 'historical' at 6 per cent.

In the non-fiction categories only one class, that of 'education', reached double figures, with 10 per cent amongst men, and all others were in single figures, so that it is difficult to say what is really important in people's non-fiction reading. History (5 per cent) and biography (7 per cent) were reasonably popular, with history apparently rather more popular with men and biography more popular with women, but the actual numbers of respondents in the whole survey of 2,000 people produced only forty-six readers of history and sixty-two readers of biography so sub-analysis of such small numbers is fraught with dangers.

One cannot but feel that a national survey of this type, extremely useful though it is in giving the outline picture of overall reading habits, is bound to be limited in what it can tell us about people's reading *interests*. For example, an obvious question is – do most people only have one book on the go at the one time? Are people really 'currently reading' an 'encyclopaedia/atlas/dictionary' as six respondents claimed to be doing? When fifty-eight people claimed to be reading a 'modern novel' what sorts of novels did they mean? And, perhaps the most interesting question of all that cannot be answered by this survey because it asks about *books* rather than *people* and their reading habits, what mixes of books do people read; do, for example, women who read romances or history in fiction *also* read biography, or are they just single-genre fiction readers only? The unanswered questions which these national readership statistics provoke are many and fascinating. As soon as we have some information in the study of the media of communication in book form about who reads what the obvious next question to ask is 'what do they read it *for?*'

Books for what?

Social scientists are inveterate 'model' builders. Often they use rather fancy words, such as 'theoretical models' or 'constructs' or 'paradigms' to describe what are, very frequently, no more than hypothetical ideas or categorisations which have little empirical evidence to back them up. If these models were a solid basis upon which sound empirical research was built then all would be for the good, since the hypothetical ideas could be tested against the world of reality. Unfortunately the models are too often devised, published, referred to by other writers and thus gradually become a part of 'theory' which has no grounding in reality.

To say, for example, that there are five types of 'gratification', instrumental, prestige, reinforcement, aesthetic and respite,[8] to be derived from the reading of literature can be regarded as either a first hypothetical attempt at clearing the ground for a large-scale foray into the world of empirical reality or it can be regarded as the end-product derived from a considerable amount of empirical work already done. The fact that this particular group of five gratifications was put forward in America over forty years ago and is not today used virtually automatically by all reading researchers would seem to indicate that people have perhaps found this model interesting and worth citing in current books on the subject, but not really of tremendous *practical* worth in conducting new researches. It is, therefore, my argument here that the 'word categories' used in the uses and gratifications models of communication theory are for the most part little more than statements of the fairly obvious which advance understanding only a little, if at all. Even with the vast amount of research that has been carried out into television viewing there still seems to be a lack of understanding of the 'why' people spend their time watching and certainly there seems to be little agreement between researchers on the actual effects that television has on viewers. With the paucity of research into reading habits at the present stage of development there are often not even enough research studies on particular aspects to contradict each other, even less are there enough to build up genuine theories of adult reading habits which are firmly grounded on empirical investigation. So at this juncture all we can do is to begin with applied common sense (even though this may sometimes be referred to as 'heuristic models') and see whether there is any real evidence to support the speculative ideas.

Probably as good a starting point as any for considering the behaviour of the reader is that of one of the main providers of reading material, the public libraries. The Public Library Research Group in 1971[9] said that these libraries ought to provide reading material for the education, information, culture and leisure, of the general public. Either explicitly or implicitly many people when thinking about books adopt this four-part classification. We find publishers and booksellers referring to educational books as a general category, with scholarly, academic and perhaps technical as further adjectives. 'Information' is a more difficult term as it can mean that people are wanting to learn but are doing this outside the formal educational structure. Many books on gardening, cookery, hobbies, travel and, of course, history and biography are read for information rather than for education. But, yet again, the categories of culture and leisure may suggest books read simply for pleasure or relaxation, but they can include the classics of literature which are constantly used in education.

The categorisations employed by the providers, mainly the publishers, booksellers and librarians, are useful enough for their own purposes. To a certain extent they are useful also for the users, who themselves become conditioned by the providers' categories, but there is a danger in all this that the producer categorisation creates boundaries rather than linking one thing to another. A simple hypothetical case (since we lack research) can illustrate this point. If a person goes into a conventional bookshop or library the books will be divided into fiction and non-fiction. Let us suppose that the customer is a man who has an interest in the war at sea during the Second World War. He may know a number of authors who write fiction on this theme and so he searches for these authors' books on the fiction shelves. In the bookshop he could be helped by a subject label such as 'War' which would direct his attention to certain shelves, but it is highly unlikely that he will find both hardback and paperback books together on these shelves. Bookshop practice is to separate these two types. But also the seeker is likely to find that the 'War' shelves contain only novels. Non-fiction may well be shelved under history, as it is virtually certain to be in the public library. Even worse, of course, in the bookshop he might find that any books on his topic are shelved according to the publisher because the publisher has supplied the shelving and the publisher's representative does the restocking. In this instance the categorisation is even further distanced from the user and there is, surely, a naive assumption that users can distinguish one publisher from another. No one, in this purely hypothetical example, has thought that the reader might be happy with a factual account of an Atlantic convoy as well as, or in place of, a purely fictional account. The assumption made by the providers surely must be that the searcher knows what he wants when he is looking on the shelves and that he would not be interested in moving between the main categories of fiction and non-fiction. Therefore walls are built between categories of books rather than paths being laid to link them together. 'Only connect. . . .'

Now the above hypothetical example is based upon a certain amount of empirical observation, though not of a rigorous and systematic type. However, I would be very surprised to find a bookshop or a library in which all books, hardback or paperback and fiction or non-fiction, on the battle of the Atlantic were shelved together. Although I can think of exceptions, for the most part hardback and paperback, fiction and non-fiction are categories for separating books, not bringing them together. Bookshops are free to shelve their books in any way the proprietor or manager may feel like and probably most of us have had the enjoyable or frustrating experience of trying to work out for ourselves where (to use a personal example) the paperback book by McLelland on Marx in the Fontana Modern Masters series is to be found. (It was not with sociology or with politics but on a special spinner supplied by Fontana.) In the library, those of us who are sophisticated enough to understand the Dewey decimal classification system can locate the Second World War easily enough under its number code, or perhaps we can remember the bay with the card 'Second World War' on a particular shelf. The point is that booksellers and librarians have laid out their wares which they want the customers either to buy or to borrow according to certain rationally taken decisions (we hope). If books are simply placed on the shelves with no forethought to retrieval whatsoever both providers and users will find it difficult to locate anything. Therefore some order is necessary for both providers and users. The sorting is done by the providers, partly for their own convenience but also supposedly for the convenience of the users. But is sufficient known about what is convenient for users to justify the present systems that are being used? If everyone in the country used bookshops and libraries constantly it could be argued that the proof of the pudding was in the eating. But with both bookshops and libraries catering only for a minority of the population could it not be argued that the present system actually acts as a deterrent to people using bookshops and libraries?

The recent bookshop survey carried out to try to discover how book sales are being lost was the first real glimmer indicating a change of thought from the provider to the user. That change of thought has not yet really worked its way through to the libraries – unless there is a study of 'lost borrowings' that I am as yet unaware of. The problem is that a reader can only buy or borrow on demand what is available in a bookshop or a library. Any bookshop or library can obtain a book by order from the publishers or by inter-library loan, but this requires a special, quite expensive, activity which both booksellers and librarians prefer to avoid if they can by judicious choice of stock for display on the shelves. This selection process for stock is essentially a prediction of reader interests.

In the case of bookshops the function of 'buying' calls for real skill since the bookseller is gambling with his (or her) capital in purchasing the goods, the sale of which is necessary to make a living. In the case of non-commercial libraries (and there are few commercial ones left today) there is no profit and loss statement which can measure success, though high demands for inter-library loans, long waiting lists for books on loan, books never borrowed and even non-use of a library by the appropriate population for whom it is run can all be indicators of mistaken stocking policy.

In my study of the reading habits of university under-graduates[10] I learned from booksellers that it is crucial to have books in stock in October for the start of the university session because it is at that time that students will buy. A book not available in October which is eventually delivered in the January following mysteriously becomes less needed by the students over a period of three months. In my sample of one in five of Sheffield University undergraduates I found that 37 per cent overall said they had never ordered a book from their university bookseller and the figure was as high as 33 per cent for third-year students. Turning to library use, 16 per cent of students said they did not make use of any library for borrowing books (particularly high amongst medical students, pure scientists and some technologists) and near the end of the Lent Term 35 per cent of students had no books on loan from the university libraries. A major conclusion which I drew from this study, which was not universally popular, was that many undergraduates seem to make much less use of books than some people believe. However, the failure rate in examinations at Sheffield does not seem to be at all high, so the system apparently works all right and no one is suggesting that it needs a major overhaul. But clearly, for quite an appreciable number of students library facilities are not really all that important and it could be argued that there is an over-provision of library facilities for undergraduates because the providers know too little of the *real* reading habits and information needs of this particular group of customers.

In the more recent study I made of the readership of 'the modern literary novel', and especially its provision in public libraries, I found that most public library authorities in England and Wales try very hard to buy copies of as many new serious novels as their budgets permit. This means that they are frequently purchasing hardback novels at quite substantial cost written by completely unknown authors in the case of first novels and often by relatively unknown authors in many other cases. Yet, in a national survey I carried out, many stock editors made it clear that they felt they had a duty to try to obtain at least one copy (sometimes more) of every new 'serious' novel published in this country by a reputable publishing house. Clearly the reader demand for such books could only be guessed at, especially since many librarians order the books before they are published or reviewed in the press. The reader demand for books by authors such as Graham Greene, Iris Murdoch or the queen of library fiction, Catherine Cookson, need never raise doubts in any stock editor's mind, but gauging the potential demand for a 'difficult' novel by a completely new author is obviously a hazardous business and might result in books standing unwanted on the fiction shelves. Librarians take very seriously what they consider to be their duty to *make available* to the general public a wide variety of books and if these should include unpopular modern fiction which is not in demand the public duty may be felt to outweigh the simple meeting of expressed demand for very light literature such as romances and thrillers. Most librarians will admit that they could probably increase the use made of their lending libraries and bump up their annual loans by stocking more romances and thrillers and fewer serious novels, but they do not do this. Their rationale for *not* meeting reader demand rests on a belief that 'culture' must be catered for as well as simple 'leisure' and therefore the interests of the minority must be catered for as well as those of the majority. The problem is that this argument does not answer the question as to who, if anyone at all, caters for the 40-odd per cent of the adult population who do not seem to be interested in reading books at all. Not long ago the government launched a national campaign to try to combat adult illiteracy. There has been no campaign to combat non-reading amongst the presumably literate population.

This brings us back, then, to the apparently intractable problem of trying to provide books for people who do not seem to want them in so many instances. Whitehead's[11] very large-scale study of children's reading habits showed that by the age of 14, 36 per cent of young people were not reading books at all for pleasure, though many read comics or magazines and obviously had to *use* books for their school studies. Reading for education or reading for work-related information may be unpleasant chores for many people but nevertheless chores that cannot be avoided. The 'reading habit' as it is often referred to denotes an appreciation of the joys and pleasures that both fiction and non-fiction books can give. The stimulation of reading as a voluntary, pleasurable activity is what lies behind most of the campaigns for the encouragement of reading amongst both young people and adults. Yet, rather extraordinarily, very little is known about reading habits or the actual effects that books have upon their readers. Writings about 'literature' and high culture *assert* the value of 'good' reading but rarely back up these assertions with empirical evidence.

Reading as a cultural activity

The general reading surveys indicate clearly enough that certain types of fiction, such as romantic fiction with women and crime/

thriller books with men, are the most popular. Readership of the more 'serious' literary novel seems to be restricted to a very small minority of people. The romantic novel or the thriller have 'mass' appeal and are frequently referred to as books which are 'marketed' rather than 'sold' in department stores and retail outlets which are certainly not primarily bookshops. By contrast 'serious' novels, which can claim to be 'literature', are known to sell only in small numbers (especially if published only in hardback format) and are to be found in libraries rather than on the shelves of even fair-sized bookshops. The former type of book is popular and has mass appeal, the latter is elitist reading for the critical few. What then are the differences in appeal shown by these two contrasting sorts of books?

In my own work–leisure reading model I have suggested that the mass-market paperback type of fiction is largely 'personal' reading which gives an intrinsic satisfaction to the reader but confers little or no social status in the reading. In contrast serious novels are more of a status-conferring form of reading in that they are reviewed in newspapers and journals by literary critics, are discussed amongst themselves by readers, and are expected to have some effect upon the reader's way of thinking. Put simply the serious novel leaves a residue, whilst the popular novel does not. Obviously this dichotomous approach suggests a polarisation of form which is in actuality represented by a continuum upon which authors and their books may be placed, ranging from gossamer light romantic fiction or the thriller to the very heavy psychological or philosophical literary novel. The placing of authors and their books upon this continuum is to some extent a subjective matter, though it would be surprising if critics were to disagree about the relative positions to each other of, say, Barbara Cartland and Iris Murdoch. Given that there is some general recognition of the degrees of 'seriousness' of an author's book, which can quite often be fairly well determined by a reading of the publisher's blurb on the dust-jacket, the reader can gauge for himself (or herself) what sort of satisfaction (or 'gratification') is likely to be obtained from a reading of that particular title. The winning of literary prizes also not only confers status upon both author and book but advertises to the reading public that here, amongst the many novels being published, is a book of some worth which could well be an interesting read.

In non-fiction the position is not quite as easy to categorise, since the functions of non-fiction (or the uses and 'gratifications') can stretch from formal education to pure recreation. To take a purely personal example, on a recent holiday I read Margaret Drabble's excellent biography of Arnold Bennett simply because I had recently read some of his books and felt that he was probably an interesting man as well as a fascinating author. The reading of the biography was educational in the very broadest sense (and it could well be used by students of English literature for formal courses) but it also gave me personal pleasure and satisfaction of an intrinsic rather than extrinsic nature. A second book, which I had intended reading for some time, was Geoffrey Elton's *The Practice of History* which I read partly with a view to referring to it, if useful, in my own lectures on sociology research methods, but also because I felt, simply as a layman, that I would like to read what an eminent historian had to say about his craft. I found the book enormously stimulating, both as a sociologist and a layman, and I would claim that the reading of this book gave me pure (intrinsic) enjoyment apart from any value I derived from it as an aid to my own work in sociology.

I have no doubt that every reader can recall similar examples from his or her own experience which add to the evidence that books and their reading mean different things to different people. I well remember a schoolteacher of English telling me that he believed that George Orwell's *Animal Farm* could be read at two completely different levels by secondary school pupils. In their early years they could read it simply as a fable and in later years, when they knew some recent Russian history, they could read it again as a political satire. All these different reactions to books from a personal, subjective viewpoint make objective classification of reading most difficult.

Unfortunately, as I have pointed out, there has been very little empirical research carried out into the functions of book reading. This is in some ways very strange, since the reader is the ultimate object of the writing in the first place, if one does believe that the writing, publishing, selling and lending of books is intended to end up with the reader. But when one considers how the various people along the line think of readers there are some guides to their actual perception of those readers. Authors write books supposedly for readers though this broad generalisation is far too sweeping to stand without all sorts of limitations. Some writers of fiction write because they cannot do otherwise – they have an almost uncontrollable urge to put pen to paper or finger to keyboard. But professional writers, as so many biographies show, must think of their living to be earned and so writing becomes an economic activity. Even academics who write scholarly monographs cannot ignore the fact that for them writing not only may confer prestige and earn a little money, but that *not* writing at all is a contravention of their contracts which require them to carry out *and publish the results of* their research.

In similar ways publishers and booksellers may be high-principled men and women wishing to bring the best of fiction and non-fiction to the market-place, but they can only do this if their 'products' provide a profit. Even librarians, many of whom in the public and educational sectors are not profit-seeking, must try to ensure that their professional services are not wasteful of public money.

Authors, publishers, booksellers and librarians then may all be said to have an interest in the ultimate readers, but their views will differ according to their positions in the communication chain and each person is likely to have a mixture of motives rather than one simple motive for his or her function. The 'book trade', which could be said to encompass authors, publishers and booksellers together, must think of markets as well as readers and it is not well enough recognised by the public how often the idea for a new book – especially in education, leisure interests or biography/history – may originate from a publisher's editor rather than from an author. To speak of books as 'new products for the market' sounds crassly commercial, but is nevertheless a hard fact of book-trade life.

So the ultimate consumer, the reader of the book who obtains it by purchase, by gift or by borrowing, is seen in many different ways by the providers. Authors write for readers, but, as the writers' support for the Public Lending Right has clearly shown, they prefer readers to buy rather than to borrow for nothing. Publishers publish for a market which can include individual and institutional purchasers all around the world and, being brutally economic, it is not really fundamental to publishing that books should be *read* so long as they are *bought*. But clearly a book read and enjoyed is more likely to lead on to further reading than is a book unread or unfinished, so publishers, booksellers and librarians have a common aim in trying to get the right book to the right reader. Reader satisfaction is, after all, the end of the line, the goal for which all the providers must aim. But to assess *reader* satisfaction is a difficult matter because there are no simple criteria for this.

The assessment of reader satisfaction

As the lines above have indicated, a book can be said to be successful if it sells in large quantities and provides good profits for author, publisher and booksellers. Lists of 'bestsellers' in newspapers or magazines can be referred to in order to find out what is *selling* well at the moment. Such lists are derived from information about sales supplied to the list-compilers by people who sell books, retail and wholesale. There have been many criticisms in the past of bestseller lists for having been based on untypical samples of retail outlets or for having focused too narrowly on books of a 'high culture' nature and ignoring, say, the paperback romantic novels which are known by the trade to out-sell many titles which appear on so-called bestseller lists. More serious criticisms have been aired of information supplied being impressionistic (e.g. book 'X' is selling well in this shop, rather than book 'X' sold *y* copies in the past seven days) and there have even been suggestions of books which have had disappointing sales being listed to try to boost sales. But whatever the criticisms may be of bestseller lists they are *economic* concepts trying to indicate (both to the trade and readers) what books are currently doing well in the market-place. High sales are one measure of the success of a book. Yet sales alone cannot possibly tell the whole story since different books are aimed at different markets. For example, a novel entitled *The White Hotel* written by a British author, Don Thomas, was reported to have been published in the USA and to have sold nearly 90,000 copies there in hardback. Yet the same book published in Britain was then reported to have sold only 5,000 copies, which was still regarded by the British publisher (Gollancz) as '"very respectable" – it is about double what an average hardback novel sells.'[12] Obviously there was speculation as to why this particular novel seemed to have done so well in the USA but to have made so little impact here, yet sales of only 5,000 copies can be regarded as very respectable for this book, whereas, no doubt, such a figure would not be regarded as respectable for, say, the latest Graham Greene and certainly regarded as a total disaster for, shall we say, the latest paperback edition of a Harold Robbins or an Arthur Hailey. The commercial success of a book must always be gauged according to the expectations of the publisher (rather than the author who is frequently too personally involved and too little aware of markets to be able to give a clear judgment). But simply because a book sells a lot of copies does not guarantee that there are a lot of satisfied readers. Some books may be heavily bought as gifts (which is almost certainly the case of *The Country Diary of an Edwardian Lady* which set a record for appearances on the bestseller lists). Some books, especially paperbacks, may be bought because people know the previous work of the author but the current book proves to be very disappointing – one could name any number of such books bought at railway stations for a long journey which have turned out to be below par for the author. Sales can measure purchases; what, if anything, can measure readers' satisfaction?

The problem is that a book can be successful in a number of ways and the concept is not unidimensional. In previous studies I made of theatre audiences I suggested that a play could be both a 'commercial' success, measured by box-office takings, and also an 'artistic' success as measured (if possible) by the reactions to it of the recognised theatre critics. Putting these two criteria together, in the form of a two-by-two square, one can see how commercial and artistic factors can operate together or against each other. As Figure 2 shows, for the play in the top left-hand corner nothing can be done, whilst in the bottom right-hand corner nothing needs to be done. It is the two other corners which are more interesting since, for the play in the top right-hand corner, which is damned by the critics but packs in the crowds, the producers may be upset by the adverse criticisms but they can, as the saying goes, cry all the way to the bank. The play in the bottom left-hand corner is the one for which a subsidised theatre or company is perhaps needed if it is to get a showing at all. The people who put it on know they will lose money because they cannot get an economically viable audience for it, but the critics and the *cognoscenti* believe it is a contribution to our culture (high culture) and the minority who will appreciate it should not be denied the opportunity of ever seeing it because it cannot pay its way.

Commercial success

Commercial and artistic failure 'No hope'	Commercial but not artistic success 'Box office success in spite of the critics'
Commercial failure but artistic success 'Subsidy needed'	Commercial and artistic success 'Everyone happy'

Artistic success

Figure 2

If we apply this model to books and their readers we find that there are some strong similarities with theatres and audiences, with the big difference, however, that direct subsidy for 'serious' theatres through the Arts Council and (to a much lesser extent) local authorities is commonplace and in Great Britain ran to approximately £8 million in 1979–80 from the Arts Council alone, while direct subsidies for books are much rarer and on a much smaller scale, running to only about £600,000 in the same year. Of course, it can be argued that the public money spent on purchases for the 'free' public, school, college and university libraries is a form of subsidy, but this is subsidy quite a distance away from the author or publisher.

Perhaps the commercial/artistic criteria, as applied to books, are better used as a way of discriminating between the mass-market and the restricted-market type of book. The authors and publishers of some mass-market paperback books are not parti-cularly interested in what the critics think so long as the public buys from the racks. Romantic fiction, for example, is hardly ever reviewed in papers or magazines yet it sells by the million copies and publishing houses such as Mills & Boon can sell ten new contemporary romances in paperback every month largely on the imprint alone. Looking along the paperback racks at a W. H. Smith or a large departmental store such as Woolworth's one is confronted by many titles in paperback which are selling in the thousands but which rarely, if ever, are mentioned in a review in the general press. Thus the commercial success is attained, not so much after being damned by the critics, but more after being ignored by the critics. Indeed, one could almost make it a part of a definition of the difference between the mass-market and the restricted-market books that the former are not reviewed whilst the latter are.

However, we must not forget the bottom right-hand corner box which gives the book which is both a commercial and artistic success – the book which the critics acclaim and which also sells in goodly numbers. A very successful novelist, such as Graham Greene, would clearly fall into this category and would be an honoured writer as well as a well-paid one. Many other writers, at their appropriate lower levels of expectation, could be said to fit into this box too because their books would be popular and sell well enough to make a reasonable profit. A well written, interesting biography or autobiography might, for example, be well reviewed and sell beyond the expectations of the publisher. In that case it is, at its level, both a commercial and artistic success, since the publishers do not expect every book to be a runaway bestseller.

The problem case is the book which falls into the bottom left-hand corner, which may be well reviewed but which cannot reach a large enough market to make it economically viable. Many first novels fall into this category because the reviewers may find them interesting and well written but the sales departments cannot find sufficient purchasers for them at £6 or £7 a copy. Just as many scholarly monographs are published on the assumption that basic sales to university and college libraries will see the book out of the red, so do other fiction and general non-fiction books depend to a great extent upon public library purchases. It is a genuine act of faith for a public library purchasing officer to buy x copies of the first novel of a new author; yet without this trusting support for the editorial expertise of the publishers such books could not be published at all.

But as a result of a buying policy which ensures that virtually every new novel published by reputable publishing houses in Britain is bought (even if in very low numbers) by every local library authority in the country the general reader does end up having reasonable *access* to a very wide range of published books. The access may entail putting one's name on a reservation form and waiting for weeks, or even months, for a book for which there is a high demand, but if the reader only wants to *read* and not to *own* the book then a wait may well be quite acceptable. And this, really, is the crux of the matter. Does the reader want to have a personal copy of the book? Does the reader particularly want to read the book *now*? In many, many cases the answer to both questions is a clear 'no' and so borrowing rather than buying is the sensible action to take. Immediacy of access to a particular title necessitates either purchase or almost instant borrowing from a library and the second way can rarely be guaranteed.

If, therefore, we consider the motives which impel a reader to obtain immediate access to a particular book we must ask why it is so important that the reader obtains a personal copy *now*, rather than later. In the case of technical or scholarly books the answer is often very obvious: the book is of great interest to the scientist, scholar or whatever the person may be, it will be referred to again and again so a permanently held copy will be worth the money and waiting for a library to order, classify, catalogue and shelve a copy will take too long anyway. User studies of scholarly researches[13] have indicated that academics do buy books which become parts of their personal collections, though borrowing of books from which only short references are needed (and from which photocopies are then taken) is an essential part of any research. But looking at the general reader for whom much of book reading is not an essential activity the position is different in a number of ways.

There are many people with hobbies and leisure interests who use books as practical adjuncts to their activities. Such people may have large personal collections of books on guns, uniforms, trains or aircraft and they buy new books on these interests on publication. These people are book collectors as well as being readers and though sales of any one title may not be enormous they are big enough and predictable enough for publishers to be able to publish with a reasonable profit margin. But more general non-fiction books in, say, gardening or do-it-yourself are not likely to have the same immediacy of appeal for the less committed reader/buyer. A new book on cookery or gardening by a well-known writer in the field (perhaps helped along with a television series 'tie-in') might well sell in good numbers on publication, though quite a proportion of sales could well be for gifts to other people, but the need for immediate access is not so great as with those people who are hobby specialists.

When we look at access to fiction, which we have seen to be the major lending activity of public libraries, the position is complex. It can be argued *a priori* that no reader actually *needs* to read a new novel immediately it is published though many people may *want* to do so.[14] The difference between needs and wants in fiction reading can be used to exemplify some of the important motivations of book readers.

Needs and wants in fiction reading

I have already distinguished between mass-market and restricted-market publishing, though I have stressed that this dichotomy is in actuality a continuum. For comparative purposes, however, and to enable me to draw on my own empirical research, I shall now concentrate on two types of fiction, the mass-market paperback romantic novel and the restricted-market hardback-only modern literary novel.

In the researches which I have been able to carry out into the readership of the romantic novel through the co-operation of the largest publishers of this genre in Britain, Mills & Boon, I have surveyed thousands of women who are not only avid *readers* of romantic fiction but also avid *buyers* of it. Mills & Boon are, I accept, untypical in some ways because of their enormous success in the publishing of romantic fiction and they are almost unique in that to publishers, booksellers and librarians 'a Mills & Boon' means a romantic novel; no other publisher (apart perhaps from Ladybird in a rather different way) has such a strong brand image. At the present time Mills & Boon publish fourteen new romantic novels in hardback format every month of the year and, about three months after hardback publication, ten of these titles are published in paperback. The hardback print-runs and sales are not, by Mills & Boon standards, very large and the bulk of sales are to librarians or library suppliers with few copies sold through conventional retail outlets. The paperback editions, however, sell in vast quantities and the UK print-run (which includes some export sales but excludes the USA and Canada) is in excess of a million copies each month for the ten titles taken together. Clearly, then, there are many people (almost all women) who not only want to read this *new* romantic fiction, but who feel it is worth spending (at present) 75 pence a copy to buy the 192-page book. Interestingly enough these romances are now usually available, in restricted numbers, in public libraries, though demand usually far outstrips supply, and vast numbers of second-hand copies of the paperbacks are available on market stalls where a form of quasi-library organisation operates with the vendors selling at one price, buying back at a lower price and so on until the book disintegrates.

Nevertheless, in spite of the availability of older titles there is a huge demand each month for the new titles and sales representatives know well of shops and stores where there are not only standing orders each month for so many copies of each title for the shop, but there are standing orders each month for all ten titles from individual women. I have myself seen, in a northern market, a bookstall where there were hundreds of second-hand copies of the romances available but at the same time the stallholder had over a dozen old shoe-boxes under the counter in which each month the ten new titles were placed so that the customers could buy the whole new range gradually over the coming month. Now such interest in a restricted fiction genre is an extreme case, but the national surveys all indicate that romantic fiction is very popular indeed with women readers and also with women book *buyers*, so it is not surprising that Mills & Boon, who for years had an almost unchallenged domination of the romantic fiction market, now have some strong competition from other publishing houses.

In the studies I have made of the readers of Mills & Boon fiction I have discovered that there is no typical reader of this genre and stereotypes of them as silly young factory girls or frustrated old spinsters are quite wrong. These romance readers span the whole age range from adolescence to senescence but, if anything, are more clustered around the young-to-middle age. Readers are single, married, widowed and divorced in proportions not dissimilar to the national pattern and in education they mirror national figures too. About 10 per cent of readers are women in (or who have held) professional or technical jobs and, in general, the ordinariness of the reader 'profile' is distinctive. A 'typical' reader could well be a young wife, say in her early thirties, with two young children and perhaps a part-time job in an office, but this is an example only, there is no stereotype.

What I have discovered from my studies about this specialised group of readers is that, for them, the reading of romantic fiction is not only pleasurable but is also functional. The women must be able to read through a novel of some 50,000 to 60,000 words (which is beyond many people's capacity) but given that ability the interesting point is that many romance readers are voracious in their reading appetites and have an almost specialist knowledge of the genre, the authors and their styles. The writing of romantic fiction requires special capabilities of authors, to be able to write in a very restricted genre (where the ending is highly predictable) and yet to be able to establish characters quickly, to obtain and hold the reader's interest from the first few pages and to be able to write a special type of dialogue. Readers are very perceptive about the books and quickly distinguish between authors who have the magic touch and those who do not. Mills & Boon's success has derived from the building up of a list of authors who are skilled at their craft and who can supply what the readers want.

Romantic fiction is, of course, escapist writing and both authors and readers are fully aware of this. I treasure the comment made on a questionnaire in the first survey I ever carried out of Mills & Boon readers in 1967[15] when a reader added a note to the publishers which said 'Between the covers of your books I can ignore the TV, transistors, Harold Wilson and the weather. I thank you most sincerely for the happiness your books have given me.' Some critics of romantic fiction claim that escapism can be a dangerous thing and condemn this genre for that reason. Yet television, the cinema, the theatre, drink and pop music can all be said to be escapist in their way. I have yet to come across a reader of romantic fiction who seems to be unable to distinguish between the world of the romantic novel and the actual world in which they live. Indeed, many readers have made the point explicitly in surveys that, as married women with husbands and children to look after, homes to run, meals to cook and perhaps even a job outside the home as well, they *need* some escapism from the pressures of real life and the easy, happy reading of romantic fiction gives them this. I have come across computer programmers, women who own shops and even PhD students who have said that they read romantic fiction because it helps them to relax after their work. The romantic novel is an adult fairy story, very much of the Cinderella type, and it seems to have a useful role in many women's lives. Its popularity is attested to by its enormous sales which clearly indicate that for many women a new romantic novel, for personal possession, is worth the outlay of a certain sum of money. Romantic fiction falls clearly into the category of books which (in the case I have cited) are a great commercial success but which are virtually ignored by the artistic (or literary) critics. It is rather a pity that book reviewers tend to ignore this very popular genre so much, since within it there are both good writers and bad, but there are hardly any reviewers who have the knowledge of romantic fiction which would enable them to write a competent review anyway.

The books which do get reviews, especially books of fiction of a serious or 'literary' type, contrast strongly with romantic fiction and, whilst thousands of words are written about the contents of these novels, and also about their authors, hardly a word is ever written about their readers. A major research problem is to find readers of serious modern fiction since the national reading surveys, which do not have a category quite as specific as this, nevertheless only produce 3 per cent of the population who claim to be reading 'a modern novel' at the time of the survey, and 'a modern novel' need not necessarily be of a very serious or literary type. In the studies I have carried out, with support from the Arts Council Literature Panel, into the readership of the modern literary novel I have established, by using carefully selected lists of titles, that what one might call 'hardback only' novels are a difficult genre for publishers and booksellers since sales are so restricted and the possibility of financial loss is very likely. A newly published author, with his or her first novel, cannot expect today a print-run of much more than 2,000 copies (perhaps even less) for the UK and Commonwealth market. A substantial proportion of those copies will be bought by libraries and very few are likely to be sold through the ordinary bookshop. To give one example, in my first survey of modern novels I used some titles which had been selected for publication by the New Fiction Society, the book club sponsored by the National Book League and subsidised by the Arts Council. I checked the subscriptions to these titles made by two large and well-known London bookshops, two smaller but high-level central London bookshops and two very reputable Sheffield bookshops. For thirty-four titles I checked, the total subscription made by the two Sheffield bookshops was ten copies. Sheffield City Libraries had bought 450 copies. One title had not been subscribed at all by the two Sheffield bookshops, the two smaller London bookshops or one of the large London bookshops. Sheffield City Libraries had bought two dozen copies of it.

Clearly, for many people who want to *read* a modern novel, the public library is the place for access to the book. Are, then, these modern novels read when they are placed in the libraries? The answer would seem to be a qualified 'yes'. In two surveys in Sheffield I checked the date-stamps of selected titles and in both cases came up with average borrowings of about nineteen times a year, which shows the books to be going out quite well. The stereotype of the serious novel 'collecting dust on the shelf' was not upheld by research. But when, in the summer of 1980, a postgraduate student of librarianship[16] working with me carried out 100 interviews in the central lending library he turned up some very interesting results. It was no great surprise to us to discover that of the 100 people interviewed, half after borrowing and half as they were returning books which included at least one 'serious modern novel' (carefully defined by us prior to the surveying), that two-thirds were women, 40 per cent were under the age of 30, over half were married (more among the women than the men), over half had either been educated beyond the age of 19 or were still in full-time education (14 per cent were students) and a third were social class AB (middle class) and a further quarter were C_1 (lower middle class). In fact, after deducting students, only 12 per cent were working-class people, giving a predominantly middle-class readership.

Some aspects of these people's borrowing behaviour have already been reported in Chapter 5, but it can be added here that of the fiction borrowers interviewed 31 per cent said that they never bought any novels at all, 88 per cent said they never bought a novel in hardback (and a further 2 per cent bought from book clubs only), so only 10 per cent of these fiction readers claimed to buy hardback novels, and no one claimed to buy more than five a year. Two-thirds claimed to buy novels in paperback, but half said they did not buy more than ten a year. When asked to say who the most popular *serious* novelists were, the paperback buyers nominated Graham Greene, Tom Sharpe and Catherine Cookson.

Trying to find the readers of serious fiction is a difficult task in itself. Trying to find the readers of any one particular title is even more difficult. Even though the titles used in my research averaged nineteen borrowings a year per copy, finding a reader of a particular book would be difficult. For the sake of argument, suppose that a title of which twelve copies were held by the library authority was borrowed twelve times per copy a year, this would make only 144 borrowings in a city of over half a million population. Trying to find those readers would be impossible.

One technique I used to try to discover readers was to put together a list of twenty novels published over a period of roughly twelve months and use this as a test collection. I asked a literary editor, a regular reviewer, a librarian, a bookseller and an author to make suggestions and from their personal lists I selected twenty titles which I hoped covered a range of modern serious fiction from quite well-known authors to first novels. These twenty titles were used in the research into holdings by public libraries but were also used on a sample of possible fiction readers. I wanted a sample of people who could be regarded as literate, quite well educated and likely to have some interest in reading and I decided that my colleagues in the university at Sheffield made a good sample frame, especially as university lecturers, librarians and administrators are mobile people and come from all parts of the country – if not the world. I therefore took a one-in-five sample of all married staff and sent the list of twenty titles to 242 colleagues plus their spouses asking them simply to tick against the titles they had read and return the list to me. I stressed, in the covering letter, that this was *not* in any way a competition and that a nil response was of equal value to me as a reply with ticks. Replies from 146 people gave a 62.3 per cent response, though I would guess that most non-respondents were also non-readers.

The analysis showed that in only twenty-three couples out of the 146 had either the husband or the wife read any (that is a minimum of one) of the twenty titles listed. Ten husbands and eight wives had each read one title, four husbands and four wives had read two, one husband ond two wives had read three and one wife had read a rather spectacular seven titles of the twenty. Altogether, amongst the 292 people reading there were fifty readings of the twenty titles made by thirty people – a reading rate below 1 per cent. The most read book was Fay Weldon's *Praxis* with thirteen readers, followed by Barbara Pym's *The Sweet Dove Died* with six. Third place was shared, with four readers each, by A. S. Byatt's *The Virgin in the Garden*, Penelope Lively's collection of short stories *Nothing Missing but the Samovar* and Raymond Williams's *The Fight for Manod*. A new local novelist, Don Bannister, had three readers for his *Sam Chard* and A. L. Barker's *A Heavy Feather*, Penelope Fitzgerald's *The Bookshop*, James Hanley's *A Kingdom* and Emma Tennant's *The Bad Sister* were each read by two people. Read by one person amongst the 242 were Elaine Feinstein's *The Shadow Master*, Pamela Haines's *Men on White Horses*, John Harvey's first novel *The Plate Shop*, Ursula Holden's *The Cloud Catchers*, Deborah Moggach's *Close to Home*, Anthony Storey's *The Saviour* and William Wharton's *Birdy*. There were no readers of Isabel Colegate's *News from the City of the Sun*, Diane Johnson's *Lying Low* or Sue Krisman's first novel *The Thursby People*.

Obviously the above twenty authors and titles do, as I intended them to do, cover a wide span and one would be surprised if a new novelist had been very widely read. Yet, when I asked the publishers of the twenty books if they would supply me with photocopies of the reviews which these books had received it was interesting to see that, not only had most books on the list received quite a number of reviews in daily and Sunday newspapers and in magazines, but also, for the most part, the reviews written of them had been at least favourable and some had been positively glowing. To intrude a personal note here, I was a little surprised to see just how good were some of the reviews of certain books which I myself had found rather boring or pretentious. Copies of all the books were, of course, available from the public library service in Sheffield.

It is also worth adding that I was a little worried about sending out a list of twenty titles of which I did not expect to find very many readers, so I added a further five titles to the list to try to encourage response. They were, with reader numbers in brackets, Kingsley Amis's *Jake's Thing* (50), Iris Murdoch's Booker Prize winner *The Sea, The Sea* (29), Tom Sharpe's *The Wilt Alternative* (18), Doris Lessing's *Shikasta* (4) and Paul Theroux's *Picture Palace* (3). As can be seen, the inclusion of Amis and Murdoch boosted the 'ratings' but even so, for an Amis book about a university lecturer there were only thirty-one husband readers from 146, giving a 21 per cent readership.

I see no reason for supposing that my Sheffield colleagues and their spouses are a particularly anti-book group of middle-class people. Sheffield has a very good public library service and several good bookshops. The conclusion from the research simply must be that interest in, and readership of, the modern literary novel is restricted to a very small minority of the population for whom novel reading is a specialised interest in which they are lucky to have supplies provided for them by a publicly financed service. High culture, by definition, is a limited elitist form of interest and the reading of fiction fits into this pattern.

The motivations for reading literary fiction have yet to be adequately researched but, apart from people already noted who simply pick novels from the library shelves because the titles interest them, readers to whom I have spoken about their interests seem to feel that the reading of modern fiction helps them extend their understanding of human life and its problems (a sort of self-advancement and education motive) but also this type of reading seems to be sandwiched between other sorts of reading of a lighter nature (the relaxation and recreation functions for people who are 'readers'). It can certainly be status-conferring to let it be known in social conversation that one has read the latest Fay Weldon book, but if the group one is in never reads Fay Weldon anyway and could not care less what she has written then the victory is a somewhat hollow one.

For many people though, whether they read romantic fiction or modern literary fiction, the satisfaction derived from reading seems to be a private and personal one which need not be shared with others in one-upmanship conversation. In my research into the reading of the romantic novel I have often found that the readers mention the way in which they can, in the reading of a book, 'get away' from the people around them, create a sort of psychological privacy and, as so often is said, 'lose' themselves in the book. I feel, although I have less evidence to support the claim for the serious novel, that the reading of a book, especially a work of fiction, is a form of escape from the current world of reality. Even when reading non-fiction, in travel or history or biography for example, readers create their own images and react positively to the words of the writers in a way which cannot be achieved in watching television or even the best of films. The act of reading is a very special thing which is extremely personal and when it works out right an almost magical relationship ensues. When this does happen then all the work of the publishers, printers, book-sellers, librarians and so on is justified in that they have made possible the communication from author to reader.

NOTES

1   *The book as a medium of communication*

1   *The Shorter Oxford English Dictionary*, 3rd edn, 1970, p. 202.

2   W. L. Saunders, 'Humanistic Institution or Information Factory', *Journal of Librarianship*, vol. 1, no. 4, October 1969, p. 206.

3   Thomas Carlyle in *The Oxford Dictionary of Quotations*, Oxford University Press, 2nd edn, 1970, p. 126. Originally in *The Hero as a Man of Letters*.

4   J. W. Saunders, *The Profession of English Letters*, Routledge & Kegan Paul, London, 1964, p. 10.

5   Robert Escarpit, *Sociology of Literature* (trans. Ernest Pick), Lake Erie College Studies, Plainsville, Ohio, 1965, p. 14.

6   J. W. Saunders, op. cit., p. 8.

2   *Authors*

1   Amy Cruse, *The Shaping of English Literature*, Harrap, London, 1927, p. 3.

2   See particularly D. Rosenberg and E. M. White (eds), *Mass Culture, the Popular Arts in America*, Free Press, New York, 1957 for what is still the best collection of essays on this topic.

3   Harold Wilensky, 'Mass Society and Mass Culture: Interdependence or Independence?', *American Sociological Review*, vol. 29, no. 2, April 1964.

4   Robert Escarpit, *Sociology of Literature* (trans. Ernest Pick), Lake Erie College Studies, Plainsville, Ohio, 1965, p. 87.

5 See Ruth Inglis, 'An Objective Approach to the Relationship between Fiction and Society', *American Sociological Review*, vol. 3, no. 4, August 1938 for a classic analysis of this point.

6 Ian Watt, 'Literature and Society' in R. N. Wilson (ed.), *The Arts in Society*, Prentice-Hall, New Jersey, 1964.

7 Peter Finchow (ed.), *The Writer's Place: Interviews on the Literary Situation in Contemporary Britain*, University of Minnesota Press, Minneapolis, 1974. Margaret Drabble interview pp. 115–120.

8 Angus Wilson interview in ibid., p. 336.

9 Richard Hughes interview in ibid., p. 206.

10 Pamela Hansford Johnson interview in ibid., pp. 209–210.

11 Peter H. Mann, 'Author-Publisher Relationships in Scholarly Publishing', British Library Research and Development Department report no. 5416, February 1978. See also, 'The Publishing of Scholarly Monographs', *The Journal of Documentation*, vol. 36, no. 1, March 1980 and 'Publishing the Scholarly Author', *Scholarly Publishing*, vol. 12, no. 2, January 1981.

12 See a fascinating article by Rosalie Swedlin, 'A Book for All Seasons – the Country Diary Story', in the *Bookseller*, 3 September 1977, pp. 1798–9, on the birth of this book.

13 By March 1981 it had appeared on the *Bookseller* weekly list of hardback bestsellers 145 times since publication, an easy record.

14 Marghanita Laski, 'Happy Endings', *Times Literary Supplement*, 8 December 1961.

3 *Publishing*

1 J. G. Bell, 'The Proper Domain of Scholarly Publishing', *Scholarly Publishing*, vol. 2, no. 1, October 1970, p. 14.

2 See Price Commission, 'Prices, Costs and Margins in the Publishing, Printing and Binding and Distribution of Books', HMSO, London, 1978.

3 The *Bookseller*, 17 January 1981, p. 184.

4   Ibid.

5   Price Commission, op. cit., p. 11.

6   Publishers' Association and Printing and Publishing Industry Training Board, 'Introduction to Book Publishing', London, 1977, p. 11.

7   See Clive Bingley, *The Business of Book Publishing*, Pergamon, Oxford, 1972, pp. 9 et seq.

8   See correspondence in the *Bookseller*, 31 January 1981 and 28 February 1981.

9   See the *Bookseller*, 3 January 1981, p. 10, 'UK publishers' output leaps again'.

10 See General Printing and Publishing, *Business Monitor* PQ 489, 3rd Quarter 1980, Business Statistics Office, HMSO, London, January 1981 for full details.

4   *Bookselling*

1   For full details see *Books are Different*, ed. R. E. Barker and G. R. Davies, Macmillan, London, 1962.

2   Price Commission, 'Prices, Costs and Margins in the Publishing, Printing and Binding, and Distribution of Books', HMSO, London, 1978.

3   Peter H. Mann, *Books: Buyers and Borrowers*, André Deutsch, London, 1971.

4   Peter H. Mann, 'Bookshop Provision in Yorkshire', a report to the Yorkshire Arts Association, 1975.

5   Book Marketing Council, 'Books in Barnsley; Needs and Opportunities', The Publishers' Association, London, 1980.

6   Price Commission, op. cit., p. 39.

7   Euromonitor, *Book Readership Survey 1980*, 5th edn, Euromonitor Publications, London, 1980.

8   Thomas Joy, *The Bookselling Business*, Pitman, 1974, p. 7.

9   Price Commission, op. cit., p. 39.

10 See the Booksellers' Association Charter Group, 'Economic Survey 1978–79', Booksellers' Association of Great Britain and Ireland, London, 1980, from which all subsequent details are taken.

11 See Michael R. Booth, *English Melodrama*, Herbert Jenkins, London, 1965, for further details of this harrowing tale.

12 L. Schücking, *The Sociology of Literary Taste*, Routledge & Kegan Paul, London, 1966, p. 101.

13 Thomas Joy, op. cit., p. 2.

14 Peter H. Mann, 'Bookselling: an Occupational Survey', University of Sheffield, Department of Sociological Studies, 1971. (Now out of print.)

15 Peter H. Mann, 'Young People's Attitudes to Bookselling', *Bookseller*, 10 July 1971, p. 78.

16 Euromonitor 1980. All details in this section come from the *Book Readership Survey 1980*.

17 A national market research survey carried out in 1974 for Book Club Associates. I am grateful to BCA for permission to quote this information.

18 In Peter H. Mann, *Books: Buyers and Borrowers*, op. cit., chapter 3, 'The Book Shop and the Book Buyer'.

19 'Lost Book Sales: a Nationwide Survey of Book Buyers and their Bookshop Purchases', published jointly by the Book Marketing Council of the Publishers' Association and the Booksellers' Association of Great Britain and Ireland, London, October 1980.

20 Euromonitor 1980, op. cit., p. 28, table 2.9.

21 Masius Wynne-Williams and D'Arcy-MacManus, 'Book Promotion Feasibility Study', London, 1974 (see Research Summary pp. 21–2).

5   The lending and borrowing of books

1   R. E. M. Van den Brink, 'Book Reading, Borrowing and Buying Habits', International Publishers' Association, 18th Congress, 9–15 June 1968, Amsterdam.

2   *Book Readership Survey 1980*, 5th edn, Euromonitor Publications, London, 1980, p. 56, table 4.0.

3   'Public Library Statistics, 1979–80 Actuals', CIPFA Statistical Information Service, London, January 1981.

4   Lionel R. McColvin, *Libraries in Britain*, Longman/British Council, London, 1961.

5   In fact this stock is held by 162 library authorities giving data to CIPFA, which leaves four authorities unaccounted for from the 166 total.

6   'The United Kingdom in Figures', 1980 edn, Government Statistical Service, HMSO, London, 1980.

7   See Euromonitor 1980, op. cit., p. 16, table 2.3.

8   Martin L. Ward, *Readers and Library Users*, The Library Association, London, 1977.

9   J. N. Taylor and I. M. Johnson, 'Public Libraries and their Use', Department of Education and Science Library Information Series no. 4, HMSO, London, 1973, p. 3.

10   Euromonitor, op. cit., p. 16, table 2.3. Raw data re-analysed to produce borrower profile.

11   Taylor and Johnson, op. cit. See p. 9 for original tables.

12   Barry Totterdell and Jean Bird, 'The Effective Library', Report of the Hillingdon Project on Public Library Effectiveness, The Library Association, London, 1976.

13   'Library Services in Greenwich', Key Issue Report, London Borough of Greenwich Programme Planning Section, February 1974 (duplicated), p. 7.

14   Martin Ward, op. cit.

15   London Borough of Greenwich, op. cit., p. 9.

16 A. W. McLellan, *The Reader, the Library and the Book*, Clive Bingley, London, 1973, p. 25.

17 Totterdell and Bird, op. cit., pp. 49 and 73.

18 Book Club Associates, London. I am grateful to this company for supplying me with data from a national sample survey carried out for them in 1974.

19 Taylor and Johnson, op. cit.

20 A. J. Marsterson, 'Users of Libraries: a Comparative Study', *Journal of Librarianship*, vol. 6, no. 2, April 1974, p. 75.

21 Euromonitor, op. cit.

22 Peter H. Mann, *Books: Buyers and Borrowers*, André Deutsch, London, 1971, p. 131.

23 See Euromonitor, *Book Readership Survey 1978*, 3rd edn, tables 6 and 7, pp. 12 and 13 for some data on this topic.

24 Bryan Luckham, *The Library in Society*, The Library Association, London, 1971, p. 67.

25 Cumberland County Council County Library, 'Analysis of Adult Fiction Issues', 1971 (duplicated).

26 Luton Public Libraries Committee, 'A Year and a Day', Luton Public Libraries Annual Report 1964–65.

27 Cheshire County Council Libraries and Museums Department, 'Upton Library Survey, September 1976–1977', January 1978 (duplicated).

28 Nicholas Spenceley, 'The Readership of Literary Fiction: a Survey of Library Users in the Sheffield Area', MA dissertation, Postgraduate School of Librarianship, University of Sheffield, September 1980.

29 David Spiller, 'The Provision of Fiction for Public Libraries', MLS dissertation, Loughborough University Department of Library and Information Studies, 1979.

6 Book readers

1 Euromonitor, *Book Readership Survey 1980*, London, 1980, p. 8, table 2.1.

2 Euromonitor, *Book Readership Survey 1979*, London, 1979, p. 7, table 1.1.

3 Peter H. Mann, 'Romantic Fiction and its Readers', in Heinz-Dietrich Fischer and Stefon R. Melnik (eds), *Entertainment: A Cross-Cultural Examination*, Hastings House, New York, 1979.

4 Helen McNeil, 'She Trembled at his Touch: a Reading of Romance', *Scenario*, no. 17, May 1981, p. 5 and no. 18, June 1981, p. 17. This very scholarly analysis of romantic fiction by a lecturer in English is highly recommended.

5 For a very useful résumé of this approach see IPC Sociological Monographs no. 11, 'The Mass Media – Uses and Gratifications', London, 1975.

6 Peter H. Mann and Jacqueline Burgoyne, *Books and Reading*, André Deutsch, London, 1969, chapter 3.

7 Euromonitor 1980, op. cit., p. 39.

8 See Alan Swingewood, *The Myth of Mass Culture*, Macmillan, London, 1977 for a useful discussion of this topic.

9 Public Library Research Group, 'Public Library Aims and Objectives', *Library Association Record*, vol. 73, no. 12, December 1971, p. 233.

10 Peter H. Mann, *Students and Books*, Routledge & Kegan Paul, London, 1974.

11 Frank Whitehead *et al.*, *Children and Their Books*, Macmillan, London, 1977.

12 Roy Perrott, 'This novelist is a sensation in America. He is British. Have you ever heard of him?', *Sunday Times*, 2 August 1981, p. 11.

13 For a very good empirical study of the user behaviour of research students and academics in five humanities subjects see Cynthia Corkill and Margaret Mann, 'Information Needs in the Humani-

ties: Two Postal Surveys', Centre for Research in User Studies Occasional Paper no. 2, Sheffield, 1978.

14 'Needs' and 'wants' have been argued over by librarians for many years. See, for example, N. Roberts, 'Draft definitions: information and library needs, wants, demands and uses: a comment', *ASLIB Proceedings*, vol. 27, no. 7, July 1975, p. 308.

15 Peter H. Mann, *The Romantic Novel: a Survey of Reading Habits*, Mills & Boon, London, 1969.

16 Nicholas Spenceley, 'The Readership of Literary Fiction: a Survey of Library Users in the Sheffield Area', MA dissertation, Postgraduate School of Librarianship, University of Sheffield, September 1980.

INDEX

INDEX

INDEX

INDEX